BC 21251

9-1-10   M S U Drawing School   Gift

THE WORKS OF J. M. BARRIE

NOVELS, STORIES, PLAYS, AND SKETCHES

AULD LICHT IDYLLS, BETTER DEAD · WHEN A MAN'S SINGLE
A WINDOW IN THRUMS, AN EDINBURGH ELEVEN
THE LITTLE MINISTER · SENTIMENTAL TOMMY
MY LADY NICOTINE, MARGARET OGILVY
TOMMY AND GRIZEL · THE LITTLE WHITE BIRD
PETER AND WENDY
Also HALF HOURS · DER TAG · ECHOES OF THE WAR

PLAYS

Uniform Edition

PETER PAN · MARY ROSE · DEAR BRUTUS
A KISS FOR CINDERELLA · ALICE SIT-BY-THE-FIRE
WHAT EVERY WOMAN KNOWS · QUALITY STREET
THE ADMIRABLE CRICHTON

SHALL WE JOIN THE LADIES? and other one-act plays · ECHOES
OF THE WAR. Containing: The Old Lady Shows Her Medals · The
New Word · Barbara's Wedding · A Well-Remembered Voice

HALF HOURS. Containing: Pantaloon · The Twelve-Pound Look
Rosalind · The Will

PLAYS IN ONE VOLUME

Individual Editions

Farewell Miss Julie Logan · The Entrancing Life · Courage · Peter Pan
in Kensington Gardens, Illustrated by Arthur Rackham · Peter and
Wendy, Illustrated by F. D. Bedford · Peter Pan and Wendy, Illustrated
by Miss Attwell · Tommy and Grizel, Illustrated by Bernard Partridge
Margaret Ogilvy

NEW YORK : CHARLES SCRIBNER'S SONS

DEAR BRUTUS

THE PLAYS OF
J. M. BARRIE

DEAR BRUTUS

A COMEDY IN THREE ACTS

CHARLES SCRIBNER'S SONS
NEW YORK : : : : : : : : : 1936

ACT I

ACT I

The scene is a darkened room, which the curtain reveals so stealthily that if there was a mouse on the stage it is there still. Our object is to catch our two chief characters unawares; they are Darkness and Light.

The room is so obscure as to be invisible, but at the back of the obscurity are French windows, through which is seen Lob's garden bathed in moonshine. The Darkness and Light, which this room and garden represent, are very still, but we should feel that it is only the pause in which old enemies regard each other before they come to the grip. The moonshine stealing about among the flowers, to give them their last instructions, has left a smile upon them, but it is a smile with a menace in it for the dwellers in darkness. What we expect to see next is the moonshine slowly pushing the windows open, so that it may whisper to a confederate in the house, whose name is Lob. But though we may be sure that this was about to happen it does not happen; a stir among the dwellers in darkness prevents it.

*These unsuspecting ones are in the dining-room, and
as a communicating door opens we hear them at play.
Several tenebrious shades appear in the lighted doorway
and hesitate on the two steps that lead down into the
unlit room. The fanciful among us may conceive a
rustle at the same moment among the flowers. The
engagement has begun, though not in the way we had
intended.*

VOICES.—
'*Go on, Coady : lead the way.*'
'*Oh dear, I don't see why I should go first.*'
'*The nicest always goes first.*'
'*It is a strange house if I am the nicest.*'
'*It is a strange house.*'
'*Don't close the door; I can't see where the switch is.*'
'*Over here.*'

*They have been groping their way forward, bliss-
fully unaware of how they shall be groping there again
more terribly before the night is out. Some one finds
a switch, and the room is illumined, with the effect
that the garden seems to have drawn back a step as if
worsted in the first encounter. But it is only waiting.
The apparently inoffensive chamber thus suddenly
revealed is, for a bachelor's home, creditably like a*

charming country house drawing-room and abounds
in the little feminine touches that are so often best
applied by the hand of man.　There is nothing in the
room inimical to the ladies, unless it be the cut flowers
which are from the garden and possibly in collusion
with it.　The fireplace may also be a little dubious.
It has been hacked out of a thick wall which may have
been there when the other walls were not, and is pre-
sumably the cavern where Lob, when alone, sits chatting
to himself among the blue smoke.　He is as much at
home by this fire as any gnome that may be hiding
among its shadows; but he is less familiar with the
rest of the room, and when he sees it, as for instance
on his lonely way to bed, he often stares long and hard
at it before chuckling uncomfortably.

　There are five ladies, and one only of them is elderly,
the Mrs. Coade whom a voice in the darkness has
already proclaimed the nicest.　She is the nicest,
though the voice was no good judge.　Coady, as she
is familiarly called and as her husband also is called,
each having for many years been able to answer for
the other, is a rounded old lady with a beaming smile
that has accompanied her from childhood.　If she lives
to be a hundred she will pretend to the census man that
she is only ninety-nine.　She has no other vice that
has not been smoothed out of existence by her placid

*life, and she has but one complaint against the male
Coady, the rather odd one that he has long forgotten
his first wife. Our Mrs. Coady never knew the first
one, but it is she alone who sometimes looks at the
portrait of her and preserves in their home certain me-
mentoes of her, such as a lock of brown hair, which
the equally gentle male Coady must have treasured once
but has now forgotten. The first wife had been slightly
lame, and in their brief married life he had carried
solicitously a rest for her foot, had got so accustomed
to doing this, that after a quarter of a century with our
Mrs. Coady he still finds footstools for her as if she
were lame also. She has ceased to pucker her face over
this, taking it as a kind little thoughtless attention,
and indeed with the years has developed a friendly
limp.*

*Of the other four ladies, all young and physically
fair, two are married. Mrs. Dearth is tall, of smoulder-
ing eye and fierce desires, murky beasts lie in ambush
in the labyrinths of her mind, she is a white-faced
gypsy with a husky voice, most beautiful when she is
sullen, and therefore frequently at her best. The other
ladies when in conclave refer to her as The Dearth.
Mrs. Purdie is a safer companion for the toddling kind
of man. She is soft and pleading, and would seek
what she wants by laying her head on the loved one's*

*shoulder, while The Dearth might attain it with a pistol.
A brighter spirit than either is Joanna Trout who,
when her affections are not engaged, has a merry face
and figure, but can dismiss them both at the important
moment, which is at the word 'love.' Then Joanna
quivers, her sense of humour ceases to beat and the dull-
est man may go ahead. There remains Lady Caroline
Laney of the disdainful poise, lately from the enormously
select school where they are taught to pronounce their
r's as w's; nothing else seems to be taught, but for matri-
monial success nothing else is necessary. Every woman who pronounces r as w will find a mate; it appeals
to all that is chivalrous in man.*

*An old-fashioned gallantry induces us to accept
from each of these ladies her own estimate of herself,
and fortunately it is favourable in every case. This
refers to their estimate of themselves up to the hour
of ten on the evening on which we first meet them; the
estimate may have changed temporarily by the time we
part from them on the following morning. What their
mirrors say to each of them is, A dear face, not classi-
cally perfect but abounding in that changing charm
which is the best type of English womanhood; here
is a woman who has seen and felt far more than her
reticent nature readily betrays; she sometimes smiles,
but behind that concession, controlling it in a manner*

hardly less than adorable, lurks the sigh called Know-
ledge; a strangely interesting face, mysterious; a
line for her tombstone might be 'If I had been a man
what adventures I could have had with her who lies
here.'

Are these ladies then so very alike? They would
all deny it, so we must take our own soundings. At
this moment of their appearance in the drawing-room
at least they are alike in having a common interest. No
sooner has the dining-room door closed than purpose
leaps to their eyes; oddly enough, the men having been
got rid of, the drama begins.

ALICE DEARTH (*the darkest spirit but the bravest*).
We must not waste a second. Our minds are
made up, I think?

JOANNA. Now is the time.

MRS. COADE (*at once delighted and appalled*).
Yes, now if at all; but should we?

ALICE. Certainly; and before the men come
in.

MABEL PURDIE. You don't think we should
wait for the men? They are as much in it
as we are.

LADY CAROLINE (*unlucky, as her opening remark is without a single* r). Lob would be with them. If the thing is to be done at all it should be done now.

MRS. COADE. Is it quite fair to Lob? After all, he is our host.

JOANNA. Of course it isn't fair to him, but let's do it, Coady.

MRS. COADE. Yes, let's do it!

MABEL. Mrs. Dearth *is* doing it.

ALICE (*who is writing out a telegram*). Of course I am. The men are not coming, are they?

JOANNA (*reconnoitring*). No; your husband is having another glass of port.

ALICE. I am sure he is. One of you ring, please.

(*The bold* JOANNA *rings.*)

MRS. COADE. Poor Matey!

LADY CAROLINE. He wichly desewves what he is about to get.

JOANNA. He is coming! Don't all stand huddled together like conspirators.

MRS. COADE. It is what we are!

(*Swiftly they find seats, and are sunk thereon like ladies waiting languidly for their lords, when the doomed butler appears. He is a man of brawn, who would cast any one of them forth for a wager; but we are about to connive at the triumph of mind over matter.*)

ALICE (*always at her best before "the bright face of danger"*). Ah, Matey, I wish this telegram sent.

MATEY (*a general favourite*). Very good, ma'am. The village post office closed at eight, but if your message is important——

ALICE. It is; and you are so clever, Matey, I am sure that you can persuade them to oblige you.

MATEY (*taking the telegram*). I will see to it myself, ma'am; you can depend on its going.

(*There comes a little gasp from* COADY, *which is the equivalent to dropping a stitch in needle-work.*)

ALICE (*who is* THE DEARTH *now*). Thank you. Better read the telegram, Matey, to be sure that you can make it out. (MATEY *reads it to himself, and he has never quite the same faith in woman again.* THE DEARTH *continues in a purring voice.*) Read it aloud, Matey.

MATEY. Oh, ma'am!

ALICE (*without the purr*). Aloud.

(*Thus encouraged, he reads the fatal missive.*)

MATEY. 'To Police Station, Great Cumney. Send officer first thing to-morrow morning to arrest Matey, butler, for theft of rings.'

ALICE. Yes, that is quite right.

MATEY. Ma'am! (*But seeing that she has taken up a book, he turns to* LADY CAROLINE.) My lady!

LADY CAROLINE (*whose voice strikes colder than* THE DEARTH'*s*). Should we not say how many wings?

ALICE. Yes, put in the number of rings, Matey.

(MATEY *does not put in the number, but he produces three rings from unostentatious parts of his person and returns them without noticeable dignity to their various owners.*)

MATEY (*hopeful that the incident is now closed*). May I tear up the telegram, ma'am?

ALICE. Certainly not.

LADY CAROLINE. I always said that this man was the culpwit. I am nevaw mistaken in faces, and I see bwoad awwows all over youws, Matey.

(*He might reply that he sees* w's *all over hers, but it is no moment for repartee.*)

MATEY. It is deeply regretted.

ALICE (*darkly*). I am sure it is.

JOANNA (*who has seldom remained silent for so long*). We may as well tell him now that it is not our rings we are worrying about. They have just been a means to an end, Matey.

(*The stir among the ladies shows that they have arrived at the more interesting point.*)

ALICE. Precisely. In other words that telegram is sent unless——

(MATEY'S *head rises.*)

JOANNA. Unless you can tell us instantly what peculiarity it is that all we ladies have in common.

MABEL. Not only the ladies; all the guests in this house.

ALICE. We have been here a week, and we

find that when Lob invited us he knew us all so little that we begin to wonder why he asked us. And now from words he has let drop we know that we were invited because of something he thinks we have in common.

MABEL. But he won't say what it is.

LADY CAROLINE (*drawing back a little from* JOANNA). One knows that no people could be more unlike.

JOANNA (*thankfully*). One does.

MRS. COADE. And we can't sleep at night, Matey, for wondering what this something is.

JOANNA (*summing up*). But we are sure you know, and if you don't tell us—quod.

MATEY (*with growing uneasiness*). I don't know what you mean, ladies.

ALICE. Oh yes, you do.

MRS. COADE. You must admit that your master is a very strange person.

MATEY (*wriggling*). He is a little odd, ma'am. That is why every one calls him Lob; not Mr. Lob.

JOANNA. He is so odd that it has got on my nerves that we have been invited here for some

sort of horrid experiment. (MATEY *shivers*.)
You look as if you thought so too!

MATEY. Oh no, miss, I—he—(*The words he
would keep back elude him*).　You shouldn't have
come, ladies; you didn't ought to have come.

> (*For the moment he is sorrier for them than
> for himself.*)

LADY CAROLINE. Shouldn't have come! Now,
my man, what do you mean by that?

MATEY. Nothing, my lady: I—I just mean
why did you come if you are the kind he thinks?

MABEL. The kind he thinks?

ALICE. What kind does he think? Now we
are getting at it.

MATEY (*guardedly*). I haven't a notion,
ma'am.

LADY CAROLINE (*whose w's must henceforth
be supplied by the judicious reader*). Then it is
not necessarily our virtue that makes Lob
interested in us?

MATEY (*thoughtlessly*). No, my lady; oh no,
my lady. (*This makes an unfavourable impression.*)

MRS. COADE. And yet, you know, he is rather
lovable.

MATEY (*carried away*). He is, ma'am. He is the most lovable old devil—I beg pardon, ma'am.

JOANNA. You scarcely need to, for in a way it is true. I have seen him out there among his flowers, petting them, talking to them, coaxing them till they simply *had* to grow.

ALICE (*making use perhaps of the wrong adjective*). It is certainly a divine garden.

(*They all look at the unblinking enemy.*)

MRS. COADE (*not more deceived than the others*). How lovely it is in the moonlight! Roses, roses, all the way. (*Dreamily.*) It is like a hat I once had when I was young.

ALICE. Lob is such an amazing gardener that I believe he could even grow hats.

LADY CAROLINE (*who will catch it for this*). He is a wonderful gardener; but is that quite nice at his age? What *is* his age, man?

MATEY (*shuffling*). He won't tell, my lady. I think he is frightened that the police would step in if they knew how old he is. They do say in the village that they remember him seventy years ago, looking just as he does to-day.

ALICE. Absurd.

MATEY. Yes, ma'am; but there are his razors.

LADY CAROLINE. Razors?

MATEY. *You* won't know about razors, my lady, not being married—as yet—excuse me. But a married lady can tell a man's age by the number of his razors. (*A little scared.*) If you saw his razors—there is a little world of them, from patents of the present day back to implements so horrible, you can picture him with them in his hand scraping his way through the ages.

LADY CAROLINE. You amuse one to an extent. Was he ever married?

MATEY (*too lightly*). He has quite forgotten, my lady. (*Reflecting.*) How long ago is it since Merry England?

LADY CAROLINE. Why do you ask?

MABEL. In Queen Elizabeth's time, wasn't it?

MATEY. He says he is all that is left of Merry England: that little man.

MABEL (*who has brothers*). Lob? I think there is a famous cricketer called Lob.

MRS. COADE. Wasn't there a Lob in Shakespeare? No, of course I am thinking of Robin Goodfellow.

LADY CAROLINE. The names are so alike.

JOANNA. Robin Goodfellow was Puck.

MRS. COADE (*with natural elation*). That is what was in my head. Lob was another name for Puck.

JOANNA. Well, he is certainly rather like what Puck might have grown into if he had forgotten to die. And, by the way, I remember now he does call his flowers by the old Elizabethan names.

MATEY. He always calls the Nightingale Philomel, miss—if that is any help.

ALICE (*who is not omniscient*). None whatever. Tell me this, did he specially ask you all for Midsummer week?

(*They assent.*)

MATEY (*who might more judiciously have remained silent*). He would!

MRS. COADE. Now what do you mean?

MATEY. He always likes them to be here on Midsummer night, ma'am.

ALICE. Them? Whom?

MATEY. Them who have that in common.

MABEL. What can it be?

MATEY. I don't know.

LADY CAROLINE (*suddenly introspective*). I hope we are all nice women? We don't know each other very well. (*Certain suspicions are reborn in various breasts.*) Does anything startling happen at those times?

MATEY. I don't know.

JOANNA. Why, I believe this is Midsummer Eve?

MATEY. Yes, miss, it is. The villagers know it. They are all inside their houses, to-night— with the doors barred.

LADY CAROLINE. Because of—of him?

MATEY. He frightens them. There are stories.

ALICE. What alarms them? Tell us—or— (*She brandishes the telegram.*)

MATEY. I know nothing for certain, ma'am. I have never done it myself. He has wanted me to, but I wouldn't.

MABEL. Done what?

MATEY (*with fine appeal*). Oh, ma'am, don't ask me. Be merciful to me, ma'am. I am not

bad naturally. It was just going into domestic
service that did for me; the accident of being
flung among bad companions. It 's touch and go
how the poor turn out in this world; all depends
on your taking the right or the wrong turning.

MRS. COADE (*the lenient*). I daresay that is true.

MATEY (*under this touch of sun*). When I was
young, ma'am, I was offered a clerkship in the
city. If I had taken it there wouldn't be a more
honest man alive to-day. I would give the
world to be able to begin over again.

(*He means every word of it, though the flowers
would here, if they dared, burst into ironical
applause.*)

MRS. COADE. It is very sad, Mrs. Dearth.

ALICE. I am sorry for him; but still——

MATEY (*his eyes turning to* LADY CAROLINE).
What do you say, my lady?

LADY CAROLINE (*briefly*). As you ask me, I
should certainly say jail.

MATEY (*desperately*). If you will say no more
about this, ma'am—I'll give you a tip that is
worth it.

ALICE. Ah, now you are talking.

LADY CAROLINE. Don't listen to him.

MATEY (*lowering*). You are the one that is hardest on me.

LADY CAROLINE. Yes, I flatter myself I am.

MATEY (*forgetting himself*). You might take a wrong turning yourself, my lady.

LADY CAROLINE. I? How dare you, man?

(*But the flowers rather like him for this: it is possibly what gave them a certain idea.*)

JOANNA (*near the keyhole of the dining-room door*). The men are rising.

ALICE (*hurriedly*). Very well, Matey, we agree —if the 'tip' is good enough.

LADY CAROLINE. You will regret this.

MATEY. I think not, my lady. It's this: I wouldn't go out to-night if he asks you. Go into the garden, if you like. The garden is all right. (*He really believes this.*) I wouldn't go farther —not to-night.

MRS. COADE. But he never proposes to us to go farther. Why should he to-night?

MATEY. I don't know, ma'am, but don't any of you go—(*devilishly*) except you, my lady; I should like you to go.

LADY CAROLINE. Fellow!

(*They consider this odd warning.*)

ALICE. Shall I? (*They nod and she tears up the telegram.*)

MATEY (*with a gulp*). Thank you, ma'am.

LADY CAROLINE. You should have sent that telegram off.

JOANNA. You are sure you have told us all you know, Matey?

MATEY. Yes, miss. (*But at the door he is more generous.*) Above all, ladies, I wouldn't go into the wood.

MABEL. The wood? Why, there is no wood within a dozen miles of here.

MATEY. No, ma'am. But all the same I wouldn't go into it, ladies—not if I was you.

(*With this cryptic warning he leaves them, and any discussion of it is prevented by the arrival of their host. LOB is very small, and probably no one has ever looked so old except some newborn child. To such as watch him narrowly, as the ladies now do for the first time, he has the effect of seeming to be hollow, an attenuated piece of piping in-*)

*sufficiently inflated; one feels that if he were
to strike against a solid object he might re-
bound feebly from it, which would be less dis-
concerting if he did not obviously know this
and carefully avoid the furniture; he is
so light that the subject must not be mentioned in his presence, but it is possible
that, were the ladies to combine, they could
blow him out of a chair. He enters por-
tentously, his hands behind his back, as if
every bit of him, from his domed head to his
little feet, were the physical expressions of
the deep thoughts within him, then suddenly he whirls round to make his guests
jump. This amuses him vastly, and he
regains his gravity with difficulty. He
addresses* MRS. COADE.)

LOB. Standing, dear lady? Pray be seated.

(*He finds a chair for her and pulls it away
as she is about to sit, or kindly pretends to
be about to do so, for he has had this quaint
conceit every evening since she arrived.*)

MRS. COADE (*who loves children*). You naughty!

LOB (*eagerly*). It is quite a flirtation, isn't it?

(*He rolls on a chair, kicking out his legs in an ecstasy of satisfaction. But the ladies are not certain that he is the little innocent they have hitherto thought him. The advent of* MR. COADE *and* MR. PURDIE *presently adds to their misgivings.* MR. COADE *is old, a sweet pippin of a man with a gentle smile for all; he must have suffered much, you conclude incorrectly, to acquire that tolerant smile. Sometimes, as when he sees other people at work, a wistful look takes the place of the smile, and* MR. COADE *fidgets like one who would be elsewhere. Then there rises before his eyes the room called the study in his house, whose walls are lined with boxes marked A. B. C. to Z. and A^2. B^2. C^2. to K^2. These contain dusty notes for his great work on the Feudal System, the notes many years old, the work, strictly speaking, not yet begun. He still speaks at times of finishing it but never of beginning it. He knows that in more favourable circumstances, for instance if he had been a poor man instead of pleasantly well to do, he*

*could have flung himself avidly into that
noble undertaking; but he does not allow
his secret sorrow to embitter him or darken
the house.   Quickly the vision passes, and
he is again his bright self.   Idleness, he says
in his game way, has its recompenses.   It is
charming now to see how he at once crosses to
his wife, solicitous for her comfort.   He is
bearing down on her with a footstool when
MR. PURDIE comes from the dining-room.
He is the most brilliant of our company,
recently notable in debate at Oxford, where
he was runner-up for the presidentship of
the Union and only lost it because the other
man was less brilliant.   Since then he has
gone to the bar on Monday, married on
Tuesday and had a brief on Wednesday.
Beneath his brilliance, and making charming company for himself, he is aware of
intellectual powers beyond his years.   As we
are about to see, he has made one mistake in
his life which he is bravely facing.)*

ALICE. Is my husband still sampling the port,
Mr. Purdie?

PURDIE (*with a disarming smile for the absent* DEARTH). Do you know, I believe he is. Do the ladies like our proposal, Coade?

COADE. I have not told them of it yet. The fact is, I am afraid that it might tire my wife too much. Do you feel equal to a little exertion to-night, Coady, or is your foot troubling you?

MRS. COADE (*the kind creature*). I have been resting it, Coady.

COADE (*propping it on the footstool*). There! Is that more comfortable? Presently, dear, if you are agreeable we are all going out for a walk.

MRS. COADE (*quoting* MATEY). The garden is all right.

PURDIE (*with jocular solemnity*). Ah, but it is not to be the garden. We are going farther afield. We have an adventure for to-night. Get thick shoes and a wrap, Mrs. Dearth; all of you.

LADY CAROLINE (*with but languid interest*). Where do you propose to take us?

PURDIE. To find a mysterious wood.

(*With the word 'wood' the ladies are blown upright. Their eyes turn to* LOB, *who,*

*however, has never looked more inno-
cent.*)

JOANNA. Are you being funny, Mr. Purdie?
You know quite well that there are not any trees
for miles around. You have said yourself that
it is the one blot on the landscape.

COADE (*almost as great a humorist as* PURDIE).
Ah, on ordinary occasions! But allow us to
point out to you, Miss Joanna, that this is Midsummer Eve.

(LOB *again comes sharply under female ob-
servation.*)

PURDIE. Tell them what you told us, Lob.

LOB (*with a pout for the credulous*). It is all
nonsense, of course; just foolish talk of the
villagers. They say that on Midsummer Eve
there is a strange wood in this part of the country.

ALICE (*lowering*). Where?

PURDIE. Ah, that is one of its most charming
features. It is never twice in the same place
apparently. It has been seen on different parts
of the Downs and on More Common; once it was
close to Radley village and another time about
a mile from the sea. Oh, a sporting wood!

LADY CAROLINE. And Lob is anxious that we should all go and look for it?

COADE. Not he; Lob is the only sceptic in the house. Says it is all rubbish, and that we shall be sillies if we go. But we believe, eh, Purdie?

PURDIE (*waggishly*). Rather!

LOB (*the artful*). Just wasting the evening. Let us have a round game at cards here instead.

PURDIE (*grandly*). No, sir, I am going to find that wood.

JOANNA. What is the good of it when it is found?

PURDIE. We shall wander in it deliciously, listening to a new sort of bird called the Philomel.

(LOB *is behaving in the most exemplary manner : making sweet little clucking sounds.*)

JOANNA (*doubtfully*). Shall we keep together, Mr. Purdie?

PURDIE. No, we must hunt in pairs.

JOANNA (*converted*). I think it would be rather fun. Come on, Coady, I'll lace your boots for you. I am sure your poor foot will carry you nicely.

ALICE. Miss Trout, wait a moment. Lob, has this wonderful wood any special properties?

LOB. Pooh! There 's no wood.

LADY CAROLINE. You 've never seen it?

LOB. Not I. I don't believe in it.

ALICE. Have any of the villagers ever been in it?

LOB (*dreamily*). So it 's said; so it 's said.

ALICE. What did they say were their experiences?

LOB. That isn't known. They never came back.

JOANNA (*promptly resuming her seat*). Never came back!

LOB. Absurd, of course. You see in the morning the wood was gone; and so they were gone, too. (*He clucks again.*)

JOANNA. I don't think I like this wood.

MRS. COADE. It certainly is Midsummer Eve.

COADE (*remembering that women are not yet civilised*). Of course if you ladies are against it we will drop the idea. It was only a bit of fun.

ALICE (*with a malicious eye on* LOB). Yes, better give it up—to please Lob.

PURDIE. Oh, all right, Lob. What about that round game of cards?

(*The proposal meets with approval.*)

LOB (*bursting into tears*). I wanted you to go. I had set my heart on your going. It is the thing I wanted, and it isn't good for me not to get the thing I want.

(*He creeps under the table and threatens the hands that would draw him out.*)

MRS. COADE. Good gracious, he has wanted it all the time. You wicked Lob!

ALICE. Now, you see there *is* something in it.

COADE. Nonsense, Mrs. Dearth, it was only a joke.

MABEL (*melting*). Don't cry, Lobby.

LOB. Nobody cares for me—nobody loves me. And I need to be loved.

(*Several of them are on their knees to him.*)

JOANNA. Yes, we do, we all love you. Nice, nice Lobby.

MABEL. Dear Lob, I am so fond of you.

JOANNA. Dry his eyes with my own handkerchief.   (*He holds up his eyes but is otherwise inconsolable.*)

LADY CAROLINE. Don't pamper him.

LOB (*furiously*). I need to be pampered.

MRS. COADE. You funny little man.   Let us go at once and look for his wood.

(*All feel that thus alone can his tears be dried.*)

JOANNA. Boots and cloaks, hats forward. Come on, Lady Caroline, just to show you are not afraid of Matey.

(*There is a general exodus, and* LOB *left alone emerges from his temporary retirement. He clucks victoriously, but presently is on his knees again distressfully regarding some flowers that have fallen from their bowl.*)

LOB. Poor bruised one, it was I who hurt you.   Lob is so sorry.   Lie there !   (*To another.*) Pretty, pretty, let me see where you have a pain? You fell on your head; is this the place?   Now I make it better.   Oh, little rascal, you are not hurt at all; you just pretend.   Oh dear, oh dear ! Sweetheart, don't cry, you are now

prettier than ever. You were too tall. Oh,
how beautifully you smell now that you are
small. (*He replaces the wounded tenderly in their
bowl.*) Drink, drink. Now, you are happy
again. The little rascal smiles. All smile,
please—nod heads—aha! aha! You love Lob
—Lob loves you.

    (JOANNA *and* MR. PURDIE *stroll in by the
    window.*)

JOANNA. What were you saying to them,
Lob?

LOB. I was saying 'Two's company, three's
none.'

    (*He departs with a final cluck.*)

JOANNA. That man—he suspects!

    (*This is a very different* JOANNA *from the
    one who has so far flitted across our scene.
    It is also a different* PURDIE. *In company
    they seldom look at each other, though when
    the one does so the eyes of the other magneti-
    cally respond. We have seen them trivial,
    almost cynical, but now we are to greet
    them as they know they really are, the great
    strong-hearted man and his natural mate,*

*in the grip of the master passion. For the
moment* LOB'S *words have unnerved* JOANNA
and it is JOHN PURDIE'S *dear privilege to
soothe her.*)

PURDIE. No one minds Lob. My dear, oh
my dear.

JOANNA (*faltering*). Yes, but he saw you kiss
my hand. Jack, if Mabel were to suspect!

PURDIE (*happily*). There is nothing for her to
suspect.

JOANNA (*eagerly*). No, there isn't, is there?
(*She is desirous ever to be without a flaw.*) Jack,
I am not doing anything wrong, am I?

PURDIE. You!

(*With an adorable gesture she gives him one
of her hands, and manlike he takes the
other also.*)

JOANNA. Mabel is your wife, Jack. I should
so hate myself if I did anything that was disloyal to her.

PURDIE (*pressing her hand to her eyes as if
counting them, in the strange manner of lovers*).
Those eyes could never be disloyal—my lady
of the nut-brown eyes. (*He holds her from him,*

surveying her, and is scorched in the flame of her femininity.) Oh, the sveldtness of you. (*Almost with reproach.*) Joanna, why are you so sveldt!

> (*For his sake she would be less sveldt if she could, but she can't. She admits her failure with eyes grown still larger, and he envelops her so that he may not see her. Thus men seek safety.*)

JOANNA (*while out of sight*). All I want is to help her and you.

PURDIE. I know—how well I know—my dear brave love.

JOANNA. I am very fond of Mabel, Jack. I should like to be the best friend she has in the world.

PURDIE. You are, dearest. No woman ever had a better friend.

JOANNA. And yet I don't think she really likes me. I wonder why?

PURDIE (*who is the bigger brained of the two*). It is just that Mabel doesn't understand. Nothing could make me say a word against my wife——

JOANNA (*sternly*). I wouldn't listen to you if you did.

PURDIE. I love you all the more, dear, for saying that. But Mabel is a cold nature and she doesn't understand.

JOANNA (*thinking never of herself but only of him*). She doesn't appreciate your finer qualities.

PURDIE (*ruminating*). That's it. But of course I am difficult. I always was a strange, strange creature. I often think, Joanna, that I am rather like a flower that has never had the sun to shine on it nor the rain to water it.

JOANNA. You break my heart.

PURDIE (*with considerable enjoyment*). I suppose there is no more lonely man than I walking the earth to-day.

JOANNA (*beating her wings*). It is so mournful.

PURDIE. It is the thought of you that sustains me, elevates me. You shine high above me like a star.

JOANNA. No, no. I wish I was wonderful, but I am not.

PURDIE. You have made me a better man, Joanna.

JOANNA. I am so proud to think that.

PURDIE. You have made me kinder to Mabel.

JOANNA. I am sure you are always kind to her.

PURDIE. Yes, I hope so. But I think now of special little ways of giving her pleasure. That never-to-be-forgotten day when we first met, you and I!

JOANNA (*fluttering nearer to him*). That tragic, lovely day by the weir. Oh, Jack!

PURDIE. Do you know how in gratitude I spent the rest of that day?

JOANNA (*crooning*). Tell me.

PURDIE. I read to Mabel aloud for an hour. I did it out of kindness to her, because I had met you.

JOANNA. It was dear of you.

PURDIE. Do you remember that first time my arms—your waist—you are so fluid, Joanna. (*Passionately.*) Why are you so fluid?

JOANNA (*downcast*). I can't help it, Jack.

PURDIE. I gave her a ruby bracelet for that.

JOANNA. It is a gem. You have given that lucky woman many lovely things.

PURDIE. It is my invariable custom to go

straight off and buy Mabel something when-
ever you have been sympathetic to me. Those
new earrings of hers—they are in memory of
the first day you called me Jack. Her Paquin
gown—the one with the beads—was because
you let me kiss you.

JOANNA. I didn't exactly let you.

PURDIE. No, but you have such a dear way
of giving in.

JOANNA. Jack, she hasn't worn that gown
of late.

PURDIE. No, nor the jewels. I think she
has some sort of idea now that when I give her
anything nice it means that you have been nice to
me. She has rather a suspicious nature, Mabel;
she never used to have it, but it seems to be
growing on her. I wonder why, I wonder why?

(*In this wonder which is shared by* JOANNA
their lips meet, and MABEL, *who has been
about to enter from the garden quietly retires.*)

JOANNA. Was that any one in the garden?

PURDIE (*returning from a quest*). There is no
one there now.

JOANNA. I am sure I heard some one. If

it was Mabel! (*With a perspicacity that comes of knowledge of her sex.*) Jack, if she saw us she will think you were kissing me.

> (*These fears are confirmed by the rather odd bearing of* MABEL, *who now joins their select party.*)

MABEL (*apologetically*). I am so sorry to interrupt you, Jack; but please wait a moment before you kiss her again. Excuse me, Joanna. (*She quietly draws the curtains, thus shutting out the garden and any possible onlooker.*) I did not want the others to see you; they might not understand how noble you are, Jack. You can go on now.

> (*Having thus passed the time of day with them she withdraws by the door, leaving* JACK *bewildered and* JOANNA *knowing all about it.*)

JOANNA. How extraordinary! Of all the——! Oh, but how contemptible! (*She sweeps to the door and calls to* MABEL *by name.*)

MABEL (*returning with promptitude*). Did you call me, Joanna?

JOANNA (*guardedly*). I insist on an explanation. (*With creditable hauteur.*) What were you doing in the garden, Mabel?

MABEL (*who has not been so quiet all day*). I was looking for something I have lost.

PURDIE (*hope springing eternal*). Anything important?

MABEL. I used to fancy it, Jack. It is my husband's love. You don't happen to have picked it up, Joanna? If so and you don't set great store by it I should like it back—the pieces, I mean.

(MR. PURDIE *is about to reply to this, when* JOANNA *rather wisely fills the breach.*)

JOANNA. Mabel, I—I will not be talked to in that way. To imply that I—that your husband—oh, shame!

PURDIE (*finely*). I must say, Mabel, that I am a little disappointed in you. I certainly understood that you had gone up-stairs to put on your boots.

MABEL. Poor old Jack. (*She muses.*) A woman like that!

JOANNA (*changing her comment in the moment of utterance*),—I forgive you Mabel, you will be sorry for this afterwards.

PURDIE (*warningly, but still reluctant to think less well of his wife*). Not a word against Joanna, Mabel. If you knew how nobly she has spoken of you.

JOANNA (*imprudently*). She does know. She has been listening.

> (*There is a moment's danger of the scene degenerating into something mid-Victorian. Fortunately a chivalrous man is present to lift it to a higher plane.* JOHN PURDIE *is one to whom subterfuge of any kind is abhorrent; if he has not spoken out before it is because of his reluctance to give* MABEL *pain. He speaks out now, and seldom probably has he proved himself more worthy.*)

PURDIE. This is a man's business. I must be open with you now, Mabel: it is the manlier way. If you wish it I shall always be true to you in word and deed; it is your right. But I cannot pretend that Joanna is not the one woman in the world for me. If I had met her before you—it's Kismet, I suppose. (*He swells.*)

JOANNA (*from a chair*). Too late, too late.

MABEL (*although the woman has seen him swell*).

I suppose you never knew what true love was till you met her, Jack?

PURDIE. You force me to say it. Joanna and I are as one person. We have not a thought at variance. We are one rather than two.

MABEL (*looking at* JOANNA). Yes, and that's the one! (*With the cheapest sarcasm.*) I am so sorry to have marred your lives.

PURDIE. If any blame there is, it is all mine; she is as spotless as the driven snow. The moment I mentioned love to her she told me to desist.

MABEL. Not she.

JOANNA. So you *were* listening! (*The obtuseness of* MABEL *is very strange to her.*) Mabel, don't you see how splendid he is!

MABEL. Not quite, Joanna.

(*She goes away. She is really a better woman than this, but never capable of scaling that higher plane to which he has, as it were, offered her a hand.*)

JOANNA. How lovely of you, Jack, to take it all upon yourself.

PURDIE (*simply*). It is the man's privilege.

JOANNA. Mabel has such a horrid way of seeming to put people in the wrong.

PURDIE. Have you noticed that? Poor Mabel, it is not an enviable quality.

JOANNA (*despondently*). I don't think I care to go out now. She has spoilt it all. She has taken the innocence out of it, Jack.

PURDIE (*a rock*). We must be brave and not mind her. Ah, Joanna, if we had met in time. If only I could begin again. To be battered for ever just because I once took the wrong turning, it isn't fair.

JOANNA (*emerging from his arms*). The wrong turning! Now, who was saying that a moment ago—about himself? Why, it was Matey.

(*A footstep is heard.*)

PURDIE (*for the first time losing patience with his wife*). Is that her coming back again? It's too bad.

(*But the intruder is* MRS. DEARTH, *and he greets her with relief.*)

Ah, it is you, Mrs. Dearth.

ALICE. Yes, it is; but thank you for telling me, Mr. Purdie. I don't intrude, do I?

JOANNA (*descending to the lower plane, on which even goddesses snap*). Why should you?

PURDIE. Rather not. We were—hoping it would be you. We want to start on the walk. I can't think what has become of the others. We have been looking for them everywhere. (*He glances vaguely round the room, as if they might so far have escaped detection.*)

ALICE (*pleasantly*). Well, do go on looking; under that flower-pot would be a good place. It is my husband I am in search of.

PURDIE (*who likes her best when they are in different rooms*). Shall I rout him out for you?

ALICE. How too unutterably kind of you, Mr. Purdie. I hate to trouble you, but it would be the sort of service one never forgets.

PURDIE. You know, I believe you are chaffing me.

ALICE. No, no, I am incapable of that.

PURDIE. I won't be a moment.

ALICE. Miss Trout and I will await your return with ill-concealed impatience.

(*They await it across a table, the newcomer in a reverie and* JOANNA *watching her.*

Presently MRS. DEARTH *looks up, and we
may notice that she has an attractive screw
of the mouth which denotes humour.*)

Yes, I suppose you are right; I daresay I am.

JOANNA (*puzzled*). I didn't say anything.

ALICE. I thought I heard you say 'That
hateful Dearth woman, coming butting in where
she is not wanted.'

(JOANNA *draws up her sveldt figure, but a
screw of one mouth often calls for a similar
demonstration from another, and both ladies
smile. They nearly become friends.*)

JOANNA. You certainly have good ears.

ALICE (*drawling*). Yes, they have always been
rather admired.

JOANNA (*snapping*). By the painters for whom
you sat when you were an artist's model?

ALICE (*measuring her*). So that has leaked
out, has it!

JOANNA (*ashamed*). I shouldn't have said that.

ALICE (*their brief friendship over*). Do you
think I care whether you know or not?

JOANNA (*making an effort to be good*). I'm
sure you don't. Still, it was cattish of me.

ALICE. It was.

JOANNA (*in flame*). I don't see it.

(MRS. DEARTH *laughs and forgets her, and
with the entrance of a man from the dining
room* JOANNA *drifts elsewhere. Not so
much a man, this newcomer, as the relic of
what has been a good one; it is the most he
would ever claim for himself. Sometimes,
brandy in hand, he has visions of the* WILL
DEARTH *he used to be, clear of eye, sees him
but a field away, singing at his easel or,
fishing-rod in hand, leaping a stile. Our*
WILL *stares after the fellow for quite a long
time, so long that the two melt into the one
who finishes* LOB'S *brandy. He is scarcely
intoxicated as he appears before the lady of
his choice, but he is shaky and has watery
eyes.*

ALICE *has had a rather wild love for this
man, or for that other one, and he for her,
but somehow it has gone whistling down
the wind. We may expect therefore to see
them at their worst when in each other's
company.*)

DEARTH (*who is not without a humorous outlook on his own degradation*). I am uncommonly flattered, Alice, to hear that you have sent for me. It quite takes me aback.

ALICE (*with cold distaste*). It isn't your company I want, Will.

DEARTH. You know, I felt that Purdie must have delivered your message wrongly.

ALICE. I want you to come with us on this mysterious walk and keep an eye on Lob.

DEARTH. On poor little Lob? Oh, surely not.

ALICE. I can't make the man out. I want you to tell me something; when he invited us here, do you think it was you or me he specially wanted?

DEARTH. Oh, you. He made no bones about it; said there was something about you that made him want uncommonly to have you down here.

ALICE. Will, try to remember this: did he ask us for any particular time?

DEARTH. Yes, he was particular about its being Midsummer week.

ALICE. Ah! I thought so. Did he say what it was about me that made him want to have me here in Midsummer week?

DEARTH. No, but I presumed it must be your fascination, Alice.

ALICE. Just so. Well, I want you to come out with us to-night to watch him.

DEARTH. Crack-in-my-eye-Tommy, spy on my host! And such a harmless little chap, too. Excuse me, Alice. Besides I have an engagement.

ALICE. An engagement—with the port decanter, I presume.

DEARTH. A good guess, but wrong. The decanter is now but an empty shell. Still, how you know me! My engagement is with a quiet cigar in the garden.

ALICE. Your hand is so unsteady, you won't be able to light the match.

DEARTH. I shall just manage. (*He triumphantly proves the exact truth of his statement.*)

ALICE. A nice hand for an artist!

DEARTH. One would scarcely call me an artist now-a-days.

ALICE. Not so far as any work is concerned.

DEARTH. Not so far as having any more pretty dreams to paint is concerned. (*Grinning at himself.*) Wonder why I have become such a waster, Alice?

ALICE. I suppose it was always in you.

DEARTH (*with perhaps a glimpse of the fishing-rod*). I suppose so; and yet I was rather a good sort in the days when I went courting you.

ALICE. Yes, I thought so. Unlucky days for me, as it has turned out.

DEARTH (*heartily*). Yes, a bad job for you. (*Puzzling unsteadily over himself.*) I didn't know I was a wrong 'un at the time; thought quite well of myself, thought a vast deal more of you. Crack-in-my-eye-Tommy, how I used to leap out of bed at 6 A.M. all agog to be at my easel; blood ran through my veins in those days. And now I'm middle-aged and done for. Funny! Don't know how it has come about, nor what has made the music mute. (*Mildly curious.*) When did you begin to despise me, Alice?

ALICE. When I got to know you really, Will; a long time age.

DEARTH (*bleary of eye*). Yes, I think that is
true. It was a long time ago, and before I had
begun to despise myself. It wasn't till I knew
you had no opinion of me that I began to go down
hill. You will grant that, won't you; and that I
did try for a bit to fight on? If you had cared
for me I wouldn't have come to this, surely?

ALICE. Well, I found I didn't care for you,
and I wasn't hypocrite enough to pretend I did.
That's blunt, but you used to admire my
bluntness.

DEARTH. The bluntness of you, the adorable
wildness of you, you untamed thing! There were
never any shades in you; kiss or kill was your
motto, Alice. I felt from the first moment I
saw you that you would love me or knife me.

  (*Memories of their shooting star flare in both of
    them for as long as a sheet of paper might
    take to burn.*)

ALICE. I didn't knife you.

DEARTH. No. I suppose that was where you
made the mistake. It is hard on you, old lady.
(*Becoming watery.*) I suppose it's too late to
try to patch things up?

ALICE. Let 's be honest; it is too late, Will.

DEARTH (*whose tears would smell of brandy*). Perhaps if we had had children—Pity !

ALICE. A blessing I should think, seeing what sort of a father they would have had.

DEARTH (*ever reasonable*). I daresay you 're right. Well, Alice, I know that somehow it 's my fault. I 'm sorry for you.

ALICE. I 'm sorry for myself. If I hadn't married you what a different woman I should be. What a fool I was.

DEARTH. Ah ! Three things they say come not back to men nor women—the spoken word, the past life and the neglected opportunity. Wonder if we should make any more of them, Alice, if they did come back to us.

ALICE. You wouldn't.

DEARTH (*avoiding a hiccup*). I guess you 're right.

ALICE. But I——

DEARTH (*sincerely*). Yes, what a boon for you. But I hope it 's not Freddy Finch-Fallowe you would put in my place; I know he is following you about again. (*He is far from threat-*

*ening her, he has too beery an opinion of himself
for that.)*

ALICE. He followed me about, as you put
it, before I knew you. I don't know why I
quarrelled with him.

DEARTH. Your heart told you that he was
no good, Alice.

ALICE. My heart told me that you *were*.
So it wasn't of much service to me, my heart!

DEARTH. The Honourable Freddy Finch-Fallowe is a rotter.

ALICE (*ever inflammable*). You are certainly an
authority on the subject.

DEARTH (*with the sad smile of the disillusioned*).
You have me there. After which brief, but
pleasant, little connubial chat, he pursued his
dishonoured way into the garden.

> (*He is however prevented doing so for the
> moment by the return of the others. They
> are all still in their dinner clothes though
> wearing wraps. They crowd in through
> the door, chattering.*)

LOB. Here they are! Are you ready, dear
lady?

MRS. COADE (*seeing that* DEARTH's *hand is on the window curtains*). Are you not coming with us to find the wood, Mr. Dearth.

DEARTH. Alas, I am unavoidably detained. You will find me in the garden when you come back.

JOANNA (*whose sense of humour has been restored*). If we ever do come back!

DEARTH. Precisely. (*With a groggy bow.*) Should we never meet again, Alice, fare thee well. Purdie, if you find the tree of knowledge in the wood bring me back an apple.

PURDIE. I promise.

LOB. Come quickly. Matey mustn't see me. (*He is turning out the lights.*)

LADY CAROLINE (*pouncing*). Matey? What difference would that make, Lob?

LOB. He would take me off to bed; it's past my time.

COADE (*not the least gay of the company*). You know, old fellow, you make it very difficult for us to embark upon this adventure in the proper eerie spirit.

DEARTH. Well, I 'm for the garden.

(*He walks to the window, and the others are going out by the door. But they do not go. There is a hitch somewhere—at the window apparently, for* DEARTH *having begun to draw the curtains apart lets them fall, like one who has had a shock. The others remember long afterwards his grave face as he came quietly back and put his cigar on the table. The room is in darkness save for the light from one lamp.*)

PURDIE (*wondering*). How, now, Dearth?

DEARTH. What is it we get in that wood, Lob?

ALICE. Ah, he won't tell us that.

LOB (*shrinking*). Come on!

ALICE (*impressed by the change that has come over her husband*). Tell us first.

LOB (*forced to the disclosure*). They say that in the wood you get what nearly everybody here is longing for—a second chance.

(*The ladies are simultaneously enlightened.*)

JOANNA (*speaking for all*). So that is what we have in common!

COADE (*with gentle regret*). I have often thought, Coady, that if I had a second chance I should be a useful man instead of just a nice lazy one.

ALICE (*morosely*). A second chance!

LOB. Come on.

PURDIE (*gaily*). Yes, to the wood—the wood!

DEARTH (*as they are going out by the door*). Stop, why not go this way?

> (*He pulls the curtains apart, and there comes a sudden indrawing of breath from all, for no garden is there now. In its place is an endless wood of great trees; the nearest of them has come close to the window. It is a sombre wood, with splashes of moonshine and of blackness standing very still in it.*

> *The party in the drawing-room are very still also, there is scarcely a cry or a movement. It is perhaps strange that the most obviously frightened is* LOB *who calls vainly for* MATEY. *The first articulate voice is* DEARTH'S.)

DEARTH (*very quietly*). Any one ready to risk it?

PURDIE (*after another silence*). Of course there is nothing in it—just——

DEARTH (*grimly*). Of course. Going out, Purdie?

(PURDIE *draws back.*)

MRS. DEARTH (*the only one who is undaunted*). A second chance! (*She is looking at her husband. They all look at him as if he had been a leader once.*)

DEARTH (*with his sweet mournful smile*). I shall be back in a moment—probably.

(*As he passes into the wood his hands rise, as if a hammer had tapped him on the forehead. He is soon lost to view.*)

LADY CAROLINE (*after a long pause*). He does not come back.

MRS. COADE. It 's horrible.

(*She steals off by the door to her room, calling to her husband to do likewise. He takes a step after her, and stops in the grip of the last two words that holds them all. The stillness continues. At last* MRS. PURDIE)

*goes out into the wood, her hands raised, and
is swallowed up by it.*)

PURDIE. Mabel!

ALICE (*sardonically*). You will have to go now,
Mr. Purdie.

(*He looks at* JOANNA, *and they go out together, one tap of the hammer for each.*)

LOB. That's enough. (*Warningly.*) Don't
you go, Mrs. Dearth. *You 'll* catch it if you go.

ALICE. A second chance!

(*She goes out unflinching.*)

LADY CAROLINE. One would like to know.

(*She goes out.* MRS. COADE'S *voice is heard
from the stair calling to her husband. He
hesitates but follows* LADY CAROLINE. *To*
LOB *now alone comes* MATEY *with a tray of
coffee cups.*)

MATEY (*as he places his tray on the table*). It is
past your bed-time, sir. Say good-night to the
ladies, and come along.

LOB. Matey, look!

(MATEY *looks.*)

MATEY (*shrinking*). Great heavens, then it 's
true!

LOB. Yes, but I—I wasn't sure.

(MATEY *approaches the window cautiously
to peer out, and his master gives him a
sudden push that propels him into the wood.*
LOB'S *back is toward us as he stands alone
staring out upon the unknown. He is
terrified still; yet quivers of rapture are
running up and down his little frame.*)

ACT II

ACT II

We are translated to the depths of the wood in the enchantment of a moonlight night. In some other glade a nightingale is singing; in this one, in proud motoring attire, recline two mortals whom we have known in different conditions; the second chance has converted them into husband and wife. The man, of gross muddy build, lies luxurious on his back exuding affluence, a prominent part of him heaving playfully, like some little wave that will not rest in a still sea. A handkerchief over his face conceals from us what Colossus he may be, but his mate is our Lady Caroline. The nightingale trills on, and Lady Caroline takes up its song.

LADY CAROLINE. Is it not a lovely night, Jim. Listen, my own, to Philomel; he is saying that he is lately married. So are we, you ducky thing. I feel, Jim, that I am Rosalind and that you are my Orlando.

> (*The handkerchief being removed* MR. MATEY *is revealed; and the nightingale seeks some farther tree.*)

MATEY. What do you say I am, Caroliny?

LADY CAROLINE (*clapping her hands*). My own one, don't you think it would be fun if we were to write poems about each other and pin them on the tree trunks?

MATEY (*tolerantly*). Poems? I never knew such a lass for high-flown language.

LADY CAROLINE. Your lass, dearest. Jim's lass.

MATEY (*pulling her ear*). And don't you forget it.

LADY CAROLINE (*with the curiosity of woman*). What would you do if I were to forget it, great bear?

MATEY. Take a stick to you.

LADY CAROLINE (*so proud of him*). I love to hear you talk like that; it is so virile. I always knew that it was a master I needed.

MATEY. It 's what you all need.

LADY CAROLINE. It is, it is, you knowing wretch.

MATEY. Listen, Caroliny. (*He touches his money pocket, which emits a crinkly sound—the squeak of angels.*) That is what gets the ladies.

LADY CAROLINE. How much have you made this week, you wonderful man?

MATEY (*blandly*). Another two hundred or so. That's all, just two hundred or so.

LADY CAROLINE (*caressing her wedding ring*). My dear golden fetter, listen to him. Kiss my fetter, Jim.

MATEY. Wait till I light this cigar.

LADY CAROLINE. Let me hold the darling match.

MATEY. Tidy-looking Petitey Corona, this. There was a time when one of that sort would have run away with two days of my screw.

LADY CAROLINE. How I should have loved, Jim, to know you when you were poor. Fancy your having once been a clerk.

MATEY (*remembering Napoleon and others*). We all have our beginnings. But it wouldn't have mattered how I began, Caroliny: I should have come to the top just the same. (*Becoming a poet himself.*) I am a climber, and there are nails in my boots for the parties beneath me. Boots! I tell you if I had been a bootmaker, I should have been the first bootmaker in London.

LADY CAROLINE (*a humourist at last*). I am sure you would, Jim; but should you have made the best boots?

MATEY (*uxoriously wishing that others could have heard this*). Very good, Caroliny; that is the neatest thing I have heard you say. But it's late; we had best be strolling back to our Rolls-Royce.

LADY CAROLINE (*as they rise*). I do hope the ground wasn't damp.

MATEY. Don't matter if it was; I was lying on your rug.

> (*Indeed we notice now that he has had all the rug, and she the bare ground.* JOANNA *reaches the glade, now an unhappy lady who has got what she wanted. She is in country dress and is unknown to them as they are to her.*)

Who is the mournful party?

JOANNA (*hesitating*). I wonder, sir, whether you happen to have seen my husband? I have lost him in the wood.

MATEY. We are strangers in these parts ourselves, missis. Have we passed any one, Caroliny?

LADY CAROLINE (*coyly*). Should we have noticed, dear? Might it be that old gent over there? (*After the delightful manner of those happily wed she has already picked up many of her lover's favourite words and phrases.*)

JOANNA. Oh no, my husband is quite young.

(*The woodlander referred to is* MR. COADE *in gala costume; at his mouth a whistle he has made him from some friendly twig. To its ravishing music he is seen pirouetting charmingly among the trees, his new occupation.*)

MATEY (*signing to the unknown that he is wanted*). Seems a merry old cock. Evening to you, sir. Do you happen to have seen a young gentleman in the wood lately, all by himself, and looking for his wife?

COADE (*with a flourish of his legs*). Can't say
I have.

JOANNE (*dolefully*). He isn't necessarily by
himself; and I don't know that he is looking
for me. There may be a young lady with
him.

(*The more happily married lady smiles, and*
JOANNA *is quick to take offence.*)

JOANNA. What do you mean by that?

LADY CAROLINE (*neatly*). Oho—if you like
that better.

MATEY. Now, now, now—your manners,
Caroliny.

COADE. Would he be singing or dancing?

JOANNA. Oh no—at least, I hope not.

COADE (*an artist to the tips*). Hope not? Odd!
If he is doing neither I am not likely to notice
him, but if I do, what name shall I say?

JOANNA (*gloating not*). Purdie; I am Mrs.
Purdie.

COADE. I will try to keep a look-out, and if
I see him . . . but I am rather occupied at
present. . . . (*The reference is to his legs and a
new step they are acquiring. He sways this way*

*and that, and, whistle to lips, minuets off in the
direction of Paradise.*)

JOANNA (*looking elsewhere*). I am sorry I
troubled you.   I see him now.

LADY CAROLINE. Is he alone?

(JOANNA *glares at her.*)

Ah, I see from your face that he isn't.

MATEY (*who has his wench in training*).   Caroliny, no awkward questions.   Evening, missis,
and I hope you will get him to go along with
you quietly.   (*Looking after* COADE.)   Watch the
old codger dancing.

(*Light-hearted as children they dance after
him, while* JOANNA *behind a tree awaits her
lord.   * PURDIE *in knickerbockers approaches
with misgivings to make sure that his
* JOANNA *is not in hiding, and then he
gambols joyously with a charming confection
whose name is* MABEL.   *They chase each
other from tree to tree, but fortunately not
round* JOANNA'S *tree.*)

MABEL (*as he catches her*). No, and no, and
no.   I don't know you nearly well enough for
that.   Besides, what would your wife say!   I

shall begin to think you are a very dreadful man,
Mr. Purdie.

PURDIE (*whose sincerity is not to be questioned*).
Surely you might call me Jack by this time.

MABEL (*heaving*). Perhaps, if you are very
good, Jack.

PURDIE (*of noble thoughts compact*). If only
Joanna were more like you.

MABEL. Like me? You mean her face? It
is a—well, if it is not precisely pretty, it is a
good face. (*Handsomely*) I don't mind her face
at all. I am glad you have got such a depend-
able little wife, Jack.

PURDIE (*gloomily*). Thanks.

MABEL (*seated with a moonbeam in her lap*).
What would Joanna have said if she had seen
you just now?

PURDIE. A wife should be incapable of
jealousy.

MABEL. Joanna jealous? But has she any
reason? Jack, tell me, who is the woman?

PURDIE (*restraining himself by a mighty effort,
for he wishes always to be true to* JOANNA). Shall
I, Mabel, shall I?

MABEL (*faltering, yet not wholly giving up the chase*). I can't think who she is. Have I ever seen her?

PURDIE. Every time you look in a mirror.

MABEL (*with her head on one side*). How odd, Jack, that can't be; when I look in a mirror I see only myself.

PURDIE (*gloating*). How adorably innocent you are, Mabel. Joanna would have guessed at once.

(*Slowly his meaning comes to her, and she is appalled.*)

MABEL. Not that!

PURDIE (*aflame*). Shall I tell you now?

MABEL (*palpitating exquisitely*). I don't know, I am not sure. Jack, try not to say it, but if you feel you must, say it in such a way that it would not hurt the feelings of Joanna if she happened to be passing by, as she nearly always is.

(*A little moan from* JOANNA'S *tree is unnoticed.*)

PURDIE. I would rather not say it at all than that way. (*He is touchingly anxious that she should know him as he really is.*) I don't know, Mabel, whether you have noticed that I am not like other men. (*He goes deeply into the very structure of his being.*) All my life I have been a soul that has had to walk alone. Even as a child I had no hope that it would be otherwise. I distinctly remember when I was six thinking how unlike other children I was. Before I was twelve I suffered from terrible self-deprecation; I do so still. I suppose there never was a man who had a more lowly opinion of himself.

MABEL. Jack, you who are so universally admired.

PURDIE. That doesn't help; I remain my own judge. I am afraid I am a dark spirit, Mabel. Yes, yes, my dear, let me leave nothing untold however it may damage me in your eyes. Your eyes! I cannot remember a time when I did not think of Love as a great consuming passion; I visualised it, Mabel, as perhaps few have done, but always as the abounding joy that could come to others but never to me. I expected too much of women: I suppose I was touched to finer issues than most. That has been my tragedy.

MABEL. Then you met Joanna.

PURDIE. Then I met Joanna. Yes! Foolishly, as I now see, I thought she would understand that I was far too deep a nature really to mean the little things I sometimes said to her. I suppose a man was never placed in such a position before. What was I to do? Remember, I was always certain that the ideal love could never come to me. Whatever the circumstances, I was convinced that my soul must walk alone.

MABEL. Joanna, how could you?

PURDIE (*firmly*). Not a word against her, Mabel; if blame there is the blame is mine.

MABEL. And so you married her.

PURDIE. And so I married her.

MABEL. Out of pity.

PURDIE. I felt it was a man's part. I was such a child in worldly matters that it was pleasant to me to have the right to pay a woman's bills; I enjoyed seeing her garments lying about on my chairs. In time that exultation wore off.

But I was not unhappy, I didn't expect much, I was always so sure that no woman could ever plumb the well of my emotions.

MABEL. Then you met me.

PURDIE. Then I met you.

MABEL. Too late—never—forever—forever— never. They are the saddest words in the English tongue.

PURDIE. At the time I thought a still sadder word was Joanna.

MABEL. What was it you saw in me that made you love me?

PURDIE (*plumbing the well of his emotions*). I think it was the feeling that you are so like myself.

MABEL (*with great eyes*). Have you noticed that, Jack? Sometimes it has almost terrified me.

PURDIE. We think the same thoughts; we are not two, Mabel; we are one. Your hair——

MABEL. Joanna knows you admire it, and for a week she did hers in the same way.

PURDIE. I never noticed.

MABEL. That was why she gave it up. And

it didn't really suit her. (*Ruminating.*) I can't think of a good way of doing dear Joanna's hair. What is that you are muttering to yourself, Jack? Don't keep anything from me.

PURDIE. 1 was repeating a poem I have written: it is in two words, 'Mabel Purdie.' May I teach it to you, sweet: say 'Mabel Purdie' to me.

MABEL (*timidly covering his mouth with her little hand*). If I were to say it, Jack, I should be false to Joanna: never ask me to be that. Let us go on.

PURDIE (*merciless in his passion*). Say it, Mabel, say it. See I write it on the gound with your sunshade.

MABEL. If it could be! Jack, I'll whisper it to you.

(*She is whispering it as they wander, not two but one, farther into the forest, ardently believing in themselves; they are not hypocrites. The somewhat bedraggled figure of* JOANNA *follows them, and the nightingale resumes his love-song. 'That's all you*

know, you bird!' thinks JOANNA *cynically.
The nightingale, however, is not singing
for them nor for her, but for another pair he
has espied below. They are racing, the
prize to be for the one who first finds the spot
where the easel was put up last night.
The hobbledehoy is sure to be the winner,
for she is less laden, and the father loses
time by singing as he comes. Also she is
all legs and she started ahead. Brambles
adhere to her, one boot has been in the water
and she has as many freckles as there are
stars in heaven. She is as lovely as you
think she is, and she is aged the moment
when you like your daughter best. A hoot
of triumph from her brings her father to
the spot.)*

MARGARET. Daddy, Daddy. I have won.
Here is the place.   Crack-in-my-eye-Tommy!

*(He comes. Crack-in-my-eye-Tommy, this
engaging fellow in tweeds, is* MR. DEARTH,
*ablaze in happiness and health and a
daughter. He finishes his song, picked up
in the Latin Quarter.)*

DEARTH. Yes, that is the tree I stuck my easel under last night, and behold the blessed moon behaving more gorgeously than ever. I am sorry to have kept you waiting, old moon; but you ought to know by now how time passes. Now, keep still, while I hand you down to posterity.

(*The easel is erected,* MARGARET *helping by getting in the way.*)

MARGARET (*critical, as an artist's daughter should be*). The moon is rather pale to-night, isn't she?

DEARTH. Comes of keeping late hours.

MARGARET (*showing off*). Daddy, watch me, look at me. Please, sweet moon, a pleasant expression. No, no, not as if you were sitting for it; that is too professional. That is better; thank you. Now keep it. That is the sort of thing you say to them, Dad.

DEARTH (*quickly at work*). I oughtn't to have brought you out so late; you should be tucked up in your cosy bed at home.

MARGARET (*pursuing a squirrel that isn't there*). With the pillow anyhow.

DEARTH. Except in its proper place.

MARGARET (*wetting the other foot*). And the sheet over my face.

DEARTH. Where it oughtn't to be.

MARGARET (*more or less upside down*). And Daddy tiptoeing in to take it off.

DEARTH. Which is more than you deserve.

MARGARET (*in a tree*). Then why does he stand so long at the door? And before he has gone she bursts out laughing, for she has been awake all the time.

DEARTH. That's about it. What a life! But I oughtn't to have brought you here. Best to have the sheet over you when the moon is about; moonlight is bad for little daughters.

MARGARET (*pelting him with nuts*). I can't sleep when the moon's at the full; she keeps calling to me to get up. Perhaps I am *her* daughter too.

DEARTH. Gad, you look it to-night.

MARGARET. Do I? Then can't you paint me into the picture as well as Mamma? You could call it 'A Mother and Daughter' or simply 'Two ladies,' if the moon thinks that calling me her daughter would make her seem too old.

DEARTH. O matre pulchra filia pulchrior. That means, 'O Moon—more beautiful than any twopenny-halfpenny daughter.'

MARGARET (*emerging in an unexpected place*). Daddy, do you really prefer her?

DEARTH. 'Sh! She's not a patch on you; it's the sort of thing we say to our sitters to keep them in good humour. (*He surveys ruefully a great stain on her frock.*) I wish to heaven, Margaret, we were not both so fond of apple-tart. And what's this! (*Catching hold of her skirt.*)

MARGARET (*unnecessarily*). It's a tear.

DEARTH. I should think it is a tear.

MARGARET. That boy at the farm did it. He kept calling Snubs after me, but I got him down and kicked him in the stomach. He is rather a jolly boy.

DEARTH. He sounds it. Ye Gods, what a night!

MARGARET (*considering the picture*). And what

a moon! Dad, she is not quite so fine as that.

DEARTH. 'Sh! I have touched her up.

MARGARET. Dad, Dad—what a funny man!

(*She has seen* MR. COADE *with whistle, enlivening the wood. He pirouettes round them and departs to add to the happiness of others.* MARGARET *gives an excellent imitation of him at which her father shakes his head, then reprehensibly joins in the dance. Her mood changes, she clings to him.*)

MARGARET. Hold me tight, Daddy, I'm frightened. I think they want to take you away from me.

DEARTH. Who, gosling?

MARGARET. I don't know. It's too lovely, Daddy; I won't be able to keep hold of it.

DEARTH. What is?

MARGARET. The world—everything—and you, Daddy, most of all. Things that are too beautiful can't last.

DEARTH (*who knows it*). Now, how did you find that out?

MARGARET (*still in his arms*). I don't know,
Daddy, am I sometimes stranger than other
people's daughters?

DEARTH. More of a madcap, perhaps.

MARGARET (*solemnly*). Do you think I am
sometimes too full of gladness?

DEARTH. My sweetheart, you do sometimes run over with it. (*He is at his easel
again.*)

MARGARET (*persisting*). To be very gay,
dearest dear, is so near to being very
sad.

DEARTH (*who knows it*). How did you find
that out, child?

MARGARET. I don't know. From something
in me that's afraid. (*Unexpectedly.*) Daddy,
what is a 'might-have-been?'

DEARTH. A might-have-been? They are
ghosts, Margaret. I daresay I 'might have
been' a great swell of a painter, instead of just
this uncommonly happy nobody. Or again, I
might have been a worthless idle waster of a
fellow.

MARGARET (*laughing*). You!

DEARTH. Who knows? Some little kink in me might have set me off on the wrong road. And that poor soul I might so easily have been might have had no Margaret. My word, I'm sorry for him.

MARGARET. So am I. (*She conceives a funny picture.*) The poor old Daddy, wandering about the world without me!

DEARTH. And there are other 'might-have-beens'—lovely ones, but intangible. Shades, Margaret, made of sad folk's thoughts.

MARGARET (*jigging about*). I am so glad I am not a shade. How awful it would be, Daddy, to wake up and find one wasn't alive.

DEARTH. It would, dear.

MARGARET. Daddy, wouldn't it be awful! I think men need daughters.

DEARTH. They do.

MARGARET. Especially artists.

DEARTH. Yes, especially artists.

MARGARET. Especially artists.

DEARTH. Especially artists.

MARGARET (*covering herself with leaves and kicking them off*). Fame is not everything.

DEARTH. Fame is rot; daughters are the thing.

MARGARET. Daughters are the thing.

DEARTH. Daughters are the thing.

MARGARET. I wonder if sons would be even nicer?

DEARTH. Not a patch on daughters. The awful thing about a son is that never, never—at least, from the day he goes to school—can you tell him that you rather like him. By the time he is ten you can't even take him on your knee. Sons are not worth having, Margaret. Signed, W. Dearth.

MARGARET. But if you were a mother, Dad, I daresay he would let you do it.

DEARTH. Think so?

MARGARET. I mean when no one was looking. Sons are not so bad. Signed, M. Dearth. But I'm glad you prefer daughters. (*She works her way toward him on her knees, making the tear larger.*) At what age are we nicest, Daddy? (*She has constantly to repeat her questions, he is so engaged with his moon.*) Hie, Daddy, at what age are we nicest? Daddy, hie, hie, at what age are we nicest?

DEARTH. Eh? That's a poser. I think you were nicest when you were two and knew your alphabet up to G but fell over at H. No, you were best when you were half-past three; or just before you struck six; or in the mumps year, when I asked you in the early morning how you were and you said solemnly 'I haven't tried yet.'

MARGARET (*awestruck*). Did I?

DEARTH. Such was your answer. (*Struggling with the momentous question.*) But I am not sure that chicken-pox doesn't beat mumps. Oh Lord, I'm all wrong. The nicest time in a father's life is the year before she puts up her hair.

MARGARET (*topheavy with pride in herself*). I suppose that is a splendid time. But there's a nicer year coming to you. Daddy, there is a nicer year coming to you.

DEARTH. Is there, darling?

MARGARET. Daddy, the year she does put up her hair!

DEARTH (*with arrested brush*). Puts it up for ever? You know, I am afraid that when the

day for that comes I shan't be able to stand it.
It will be too exciting.   My poor heart, Margaret.

MARGARET (*rushing at him*). No, no, it will
be lucky you, for it isn't to be a bit like that.
I am to be a girl and woman day about for the
first year. You will never know which I am
till you look at my hair. And even then you
won't know, for if it is down I shall put it up,
and if it is up I shall put it down. And so my
Daddy will gradually get used to the idea.

DEARTH (*wryly*). I see you have been thinking
it out.

MARGARET (*gleaming*). I have been doing
more than that. Shut your eyes, Dad, and I
shall give you a glimpse into the future.

DEARTH. I don't know that I want that:
the present is so good.

MARGARET. Shut your eyes, please.

DEARTH. No, Margaret.

MARGARET. Please, Daddy.

DEARTH. Oh, all right.   They are shut.

MARGARET. Don't open them till I tell you.
What finger is that?

DEARTH. The dirty one.

MARGARET (*on her knees among the leaves*).
Daddy, now I am putting up my hair. I have
got such a darling of a mirror. It is such a
darling mirror I 've got, Dad. Dad, don't look.
I shall tell you about it. It is a little pool of
water. I wish we could take it home and hang
it up. Of course the moment my hair is up
there will be other changes also; for instance,
I shall talk quite differently.

DEARTH. Pooh. Where are my matches,
dear?

MARGARET. Top pocket, waistcoat.

DEARTH (*trying to light his pipe in darkness*).
You were meaning to frighten me just now.

MARGARET. No. I am just preparing you.
You see, darling, I can't call you Dad when my
hair is up. I think I shall call you Parent.

(*He growls.*)

Parent dear, do you remember the days when
your Margaret was a slip of a girl, and sat on
your knee? How foolish we were, Parent, in
those distant days.

DEARTH. Shut up, Margaret.

MARGARET. Now I must be more distant to

you; more like a boy who could not sit on your knee any more.

DEARTH. See here, I want to go on painting. Shall I look now?

MARGARET. I am not quite sure whether I want you to. It makes such a difference. Perhaps you won't know me. Even the pool is looking a little scared. (*The change in her voice makes him open his eyes quickly. She confronts him shyly.*) What do you think? Will I do?

DEARTH. Stand still, dear, and let me look my fill. The Margaret that is to be.

MARGARET (*the change in his voice falling clammy on her*). You 'll see me often enough, Daddy, like this, so you don't need to look your fill. You are looking as long as if this were to be the only time.

DEARTH (*with an odd tremor*). Was I? Surely it isn't to be that.

MARGARET. Be gay, Dad. (*Bumping into him and round him and over him.*) You will be sick of Margaret with her hair up before you are done with her.

DEARTH. I expect so.

MARGARET. Shut up, Daddy. (*She waggles her head, and down comes her hair.*) Daddy, I know what you are thinking of. You are thinking what a handful she is going to be.

DEARTH. Well, I guess she is.

MARGARET (*surveying him from another angle*). Now you are thinking about—about my being in love some day.

DEARTH (*with unnecessary warmth*). Rot!

MARGARET (*reassuringly*). I won't, you know; no, never. Oh, I have quite decided, so don't be afraid. (*Disordering his hair.*) Will you hate him at first, Daddy? Daddy, will you hate him? Will you hate him, Daddy?

DEARTH (*at work*). Whom?

MARGARET. Well, if there was?

DEARTH. If there was what, darling?

MARGARET. You know the kind of thing I mean, quite well. Would you hate him at first?

DEARTH. I hope not. I should want to strangle him, but I wouldn't hate him.

MARGARET. *I* would. That is to say, if I liked him.

DEARTH. If you liked him how could you hate him?

MARGARET. For daring!

DEARTH. Daring what?

MARGARET. You know. (*Sighing.*) But of course I shall have no say in the matter. You will do it all. You do everything for me.

DEARTH (*with a groan*). I can't help it.

MARGARET. You will even write my love-letters, if I ever have any to write, which I won't.

DEARTH (*ashamed*). Surely to goodness, Margaret, I will leave you alone to do that!

MARGARET. Not you; you will try to, but you won't be able.

DEARTH (*in a hopeless attempt at self-defence*). I want you, you see, to do everything exquisitely. I do wish I could leave you to do things a little more for yourself. I suppose it's owing to my having had to be father and mother both. I knew nothing practically about the bringing up of children, and of course I couldn't trust you to a nurse.

MARGARET (*severely*). Not you; so sure you could do it better yourself. That's you all over. Daddy, do you remember how you taught me to balance a biscuit on my nose, like a puppy?

DEARTH (*sadly*). Did I?

MARGARET. You called me Rover.

DEARTH. I deny that.

MARGARET. And when you said 'snap' I caught the biscuit in my mouth.

DEARTH. Horrible!

MARGARET (*gleaming*). Daddy, I can do it still! (*Putting a biscuit on her nose.*) Here is the last of my supper. Say 'snap,' Daddy.

DEARTH. Not I.

MARGARET. Say 'snap,' please.

DEARTH. I refuse.

MARGARET. Daddy!

DEARTH. Snap.

(*She catches the biscuit in her mouth.*)

Let that be the last time, Margaret.

MARGARET. Except just once more. I don't mean now, but when my hair is really up. If I should ever have a—a Margaret of my own, come in and see me, Daddy, in my white bed, and say 'snap'—and I'll have the biscuit ready.

DEARTH (*turning away his head*). Right O.

MARGARET. Dad, if I ever should marry, not that I will but if I should—at the marriage ceremony will you let me be the one who says 'I do'?

DEARTH. I suppose I deserve this.

MARGARET (*coaxingly*). You think I'm pretty, don't you, Dad, whatever other people say?

DEARTH. Not so bad.

MARGARET. I *know* I have nice ears.

DEARTH. They are all right now, but I had to work on them for months.

MARGARET. You don't mean to say that you did my *ears*?

DEARTH. Rather!

MARGARET (*grown humble*). My dimple is my own.

DEARTH. I am glad you think so. I wore out the point of my little finger over that dimple.

MARGARET. Even my dimple! Have I anything that is really mine? A bit of my nose or anything?

DEARTH. When you were a babe you had a laugh that was all your own.

MARGARET. Haven't I it now?

DEARTH. It 's gone. (*He looks ruefully at her.*) I 'll tell you how it went. We were fishing in a stream—that is to say, I was wading and you were sitting on my shoulders holding the rod. We didn't catch anything. Somehow or another—I can't think how I did it—you irritated me, and I answered you sharply.

MARGARET (*gasping*). I can't believe that.

DEARTH. Yes, it sounds extraordinary, but I did. It gave you a shock, and, for the moment, the world no longer seemed a safe place to you; your faith in me had always made it safe till then. You were suddenly not even sure of your bread and butter, and a frightened tear came to your eyes. I was in a nice state about it I can tell you. (*He is in a nice state about it still.*)

MARGARET. Silly! (*Bewildered.*) But what has that to do with my laugh, Daddy?

DEARTH. The laugh that children are born with lasts just so long as they have perfect faith. To think that it was I who robbed you of yours!

MARGARET. Don't, dear. I am sure the laugh

just went off with the tear to comfort it, and
they have been playing about that stream ever
since. They have quite forgotten us, so why
should we remember them? Cheeky little beasts!
Shall I tell you my farthest back recollection?
(*In some awe.*) I remember the first time I
saw the stars. I had never seen night, and
then I saw it and the stars together. Crack-
in-my-eye-Tommy, it isn't every one who can
boast of such a lovely, lovely recollection for
their earliest, is it?

DEARTH. I was determined your earliest should
be a good one.

MARGARET (*blankly*). Do you mean to say
you planned it?

DEARTH. Rather! Most people's earliest recollection is of some trivial thing; how they cut
their finger, or lost a piece of string. I was
resolved my Margaret's should be something
bigger. I was poor, but I could give her the
stars.

MARGARET (*clutching him round the legs*). Oh,
how you love me, Daddikins.

DEARTH. Yes, I do, rather.

(*A vagrant woman has wandered in their
direction, one whom the shrill winds of life
have lashed and bled; here and there ragged
graces still cling to her, and unruly passion
smoulders, but she, once a dear fierce rebel
with eyes of storm, is now first of all a
whimperer. She and they meet as strangers.*)

MARGARET (*nicely, as becomes an artist's
daughter*). Good evening.

ALICE. Good evening, Missy; evening, Mister.

DEARTH (*seeing that her eyes search the ground*).
Lost anything?

ALICE. Sometimes when the tourists have
had their sandwiches there are bits left over, and
they squeeze them between the roots to keep the
place tidy. I am looking for bits.

DEARTH. You don't tell me you are as hungry
as that?

ALICE (*with spirit*). Try me. (*Strange that he
should not know that once loved husky voice.*)

MARGARET (*rushing at her father and feeling all
his pockets*). Daddy, that was my last biscuit!

DEARTH. We must think of something else.

MARGARET (*taking her hand*). Yes, wait a bit, we are sure to think of something. Daddy, think of something.

ALICE (*sharply*). Your father doesn't like you to touch the likes of me.

MARGARET. Oh yes, he does. (*Defiantly.*) And if he didn't, I'd do it all the same. This is a bit of *myself*, daddy.

DEARTH. That is all you know.

ALICE (*whining*). You needn't be angry with her, Mister; I'm all right.

DEARTH. I am not angry with her; I am very sorry for you.

ALICE (*flaring*). If I had my rights, I would be as good as you—and better.

DEARTH. I daresay.

ALICE. I have had men-servants and a motorcar.

DEARTH. Margaret and I never rose to that.

MARGARET (*stung*). I have been in a taxi several times, and Dad often gets telegrams.

DEARTH. Margaret!

MARGARET. I'm sorry I boasted.

ALICE. That's nothing. I have a town house —at least I had . . . At any rate he said there was a town house.

MARGARET (*interested*). Fancy his not knowing for certain.

ALICE. The Honourable Mrs. Finch-Fallowe —that's who I am.

MARGARET (*cordially*). It's a lovely name.

ALICE. Curse him.

MARGARET. Don't you like him?

DEARTH. We won't go into that. I have nothing to do with your past, but I wish we had some food to offer you.

ALICE. You haven't a flask?

DEARTH. No, I don't take anything myself. But let me see. . . .

MARGARET (*sparkling*). I know! You said we had five pounds. (*To the needy one.*) Would you like five pounds?

DEARTH. Darling, don't be stupid; we haven't paid our bill at the inn.

ALICE (*with bravado*). All right; I never asked you for anything.

DEARTH. Don't take me up in that way: I

have had my ups and downs myself. Here is ten bob and welcome.

(*He surreptitiously slips a coin into* MAR-GARET'S *hand.*)

MARGARET. And I have half a crown. It is quite easy for us. Dad will be getting another fiver any day. You can't think how exciting it is when the fiver comes in; we dance and then we run out and buy chops.

DEARTH. Margaret!

ALICE. It's kind of you. I'm richer this minute than I have been for many a day.

DEARTH. It's nothing; I am sure you would do the same for us.

ALICE. I wish I was as sure.

DEARTH. Of course you would. Glad to be of any help. Get some victuals as quickly as you can. Best of wishes, ma'am, and may your luck change.

ALICE. Same to you, and may yours go on.

MARGARET. Good-night.

ALICE. What is her name, Mister?

DEARTH (*who has returned to his easel*). Margaret.

ALICE. Margaret. You drew something good out of the lucky bag when you got her, Mister.

DEARTH. Yes.

ALICE. Take care of her; they are easily lost.

(*She shuffles away.*)

DEARTH. Poor soul. I expect she has had a rough time, and that some man is to blame for it—partly, at any rate. (*Restless.*) That woman rather affects me, Margaret; I don't know why. Didn't you like her husky voice? (*He goes on painting.*) I say, Margaret, we lucky ones, let's swear always to be kind to people who are down on their luck, and then when we are kind let's be a little kinder.

MARGARET (*gleefully*). Yes, let's.

DEARTH. Margaret, always feel sorry for the failures, the ones who are always failures—especially in my sort of calling. Wouldn't it be lovely, to turn them on the thirty-ninth year of failure into glittering successes?

MARGARET. Topping.

DEARTH. Topping.

MARGARET. Oh, topping. How could we do it, Dad?

DEARTH. By letter. 'To poor old Tom Broken Heart, Top Attic, Garret Chambers, S.E.—'DEAR SIR,—His Majesty has been graciously pleased to purchase your superb picture of Marlow Ferry.'

MARGARET. '*P.S.*—I am sending the money in a sack so as you can hear it chink.'

DEARTH. What could we do for our friend who passed just now? I can't get her out of my head.

MARGARET. You have made me forget her, (*Plaintively.*) Dad, I didn't like it.

DEARTH. Didn't like what, dear?

MARGARET (*shuddering*). I didn't like her saying that about your losing me.

DEARTH (*the one thing of which he is sure*). I shan't lose you.

MARGARET (*hugging his arm*). It would be hard for me if you lost me, but it would be worse for you. I don't know how I know that, but I do know it. What would you do without me?

DEARTH (*almost sharply*). Don't talk like that, dear. It is wicked and stupid, and naughty. Somehow that poor woman—I won't paint any more to-night.

MARGARET. Let's get out of the wood; it frightens me.

DEARTH. And you loved it a moment ago. Hullo! (*He has seen a distant blurred light in the wood, apparently from a window.*) I hadn't noticed there was a house there.

MARGARET (*tingling*). Daddy, I feel sure there wasn't a house there!

DEARTH. Goose. It is just that we didn't look: our old way of letting the world go hang; so interested in ourselves. Nice behaviour for people who have been boasting about what they would do for other people. Now I see what I ought to do.

MARGARET. Let's get out of the wood.

DEARTH. Yes, but my idea first. It is to rouse these people and get food from them for the husky one.

MARGARET (*clinging to him*). She is too far away now.

DEARTH. I can overtake her.

MARGARET (*in a frenzy*). Don't go into that house, Daddy! I don't know why it is, but I am afraid of that house!

(*He waggles a reproving finger at her.*)

DEARTH. There is a kiss for each moment until I come back.

(*She wipes them from her face.*)

Oh, naughty, go and stand in the corner.

(*She stands against a tree but she stamps her foot.*)

Who has got a nasty temper!

(*She tries hard not to smile, but she smiles and he smiles, and they make comic faces at each other, as they have done in similar circumstances since she first opened her eyes.*)

I shall be back before you can count a hundred.

(*He goes off humming his song so that she may still hear him when he is lost to sight; all just as so often before. She tries dutifully to count her hundred, but the wood grows dark and soon she is afraid again.*)

*She runs from tree to tree calling to her
Daddy. We begin to lose her among the
shadows.)*

MARGARET (*out of the impalpable that is carrying her away*). Daddy, come back; I don't want
to be a might-have-been.

ACT III

ACT III

*Lob's room has gone very dark as it sits up awaiting
the possible return of the adventurers. The curtains
are drawn, so that no light comes from outside. There
is a tapping on the window, and anon two intruders
are stealing about the floor, with muffled cries when
they meet unexpectedly. They find the switch and are
revealed as Purdie and his Mabel. Something has
happened to them as they emerged from the wood, but
it is so superficial that neither notices it: they are again
in the evening dress in which they had left the house.
But they are still being led by that strange humour of
the blood.*

MABEL (*looking around her curiously*). A
pretty little room; I wonder who is the owner?

PURDIE. It doesn't matter; the great thing
is that we have escaped Joanna.

MABEL. Jack, look, a man!

(The term may not be happily chosen, but the person indicated is LOB *curled up on his chair by a dead fire. The last look on his face before he fell asleep having been a leery one it is still there.)*

PURDIE. He is asleep.

MABEL. Do you know him?

PURDIE. Not I. Excuse me, sir, Hi! *(No shaking, however, wakens the sleeper.)*

MABEL. Darling, how extraordinary.

PURDIE *(always considerate)*. After all, precious, have we any right to wake up a stranger, just to tell him that we are runaways hiding in his house?

MABEL *(who comes of a good family)*. I think he would expect it of us.

PURDIE *(after trying again)*. There is no budging him.

MABEL *(appeased)*. At any rate, we have done the civil thing.

(She has now time to regard the room more attentively, including the tray of coffee cups which MATEY *had left on the table in a not unimportant moment of his history.)*

There have evidently been people here, but they haven't drunk their coffee. Ugh! cold as a deserted egg in a bird's nest. Jack, if you were a clever detective you could construct those people out of their neglected coffee cups. I wonder who they are and what has spirited them away?

PURDIE. Perhaps they have only gone to bed. Ought we to knock them up?

MABEL (*after considering what her mother would have done*). I think not, dear. I suppose we have run away, Jack—meaning to?

PURDIE (*with the sturdiness that weaker vessels adore*). Irrevocably. Mabel, if the dog-like devotion of a lifetime. . . . (*He becomes conscious that something has happened to* LOB's *leer. It has not left his face but it has shifted.*) He is not shamming, do you think?

MABEL. Shake him again.

PURDIE (*after shaking him*). It's all right. Mabel, if the dog-like devotion of a lifetime . . .

MABEL. Poor little Joanna! Still, if a woman insists on being a pendulum round a man's neck . . .

PURDIE. Do give me a chance, Mabel. If
the dog-like devotion of a lifetime . . .

(JOANNA *comes through the curtains so
inopportunely that for the moment he is
almost pettish.*)

May I say, this is just a little too much, Joanna!

JOANNA (*unconscious as they of her return to
her dinner gown*). So, sweet husband, your soul is
still walking alone, is it?

MABEL (*who hates coarseness of any kind*).
How can you sneak about in this way, Joanna?
Have you no pride?

JOANNA (*dashing away a tear*). Please to
address me as Mrs. Purdie, madam. (*She sees
LOB.*) Who is this man?

PURDIE. We don't know; and there is no
waking him. You can try, if you like.

(*Failing to rouse him* JOANNA *makes a third
at table. They are all a little inconse-
quential, as if there were still some moonshine in their hair.*)

JOANNA. You were saying something about
the devotion of a lifetime; please go on.

PURDIE (*diffidently*). I don't like to before you,
Joanna.

JOANNA (*becoming coarse again*). Oh, don't mind me.

PURDIE (*looking like a note of interrogation*). I should certainly like to say it.

MABEL (*loftily*). And I shall be proud to hear it.

PURDIE. I should have liked to spare you this, Joanna; you wouldn't put your hands over your ears?

JOANNA (*alas*). No, sir.

MABEL. Fie, Joanna. Surely a wife's natural delicacy . . .

PURDIE (*severely*). As you take it in that spirit, Joanna, I can proceed with a clear conscience. If the dog-like devotion of a lifetime— (*He reels a little, staring at* LOB, *over whose face the leer has been wandering like an insect.*)

MABEL. Did he move?

PURDIE. It isn't that. I am feeling—very funny. Did one of you tap me just now on the forehead?

> (*Their hands also have gone to their foreheads.*)

MABEL. I think I have been in this room before.

PURDIE (*flinching*). There is something coming rushing back to me.

MABEL. I seem to know that coffee set. If I do, the lid of the milk jug is chipped. It is!

JOANNA. I can't remember this man's name; but I am sure it begins with L.

MABEL. Lob.

PURDIE. Lob.

JOANNA. Lob.

PURDIE. Mabel, your dress?

MABEL (*beholding it*). How on earth . . . ?

JOANNA. My dress! (*To* PURDIE.) You were in knickerbockers in the wood.

PURDIE. And so I am now. (*He sees he is not.*) Where did I change? The wood! Let me think. The wood . . . the wood, certainly. But the wood wasn't the wood.

JOANNA (*revolving like one in pursuit*). My head is going round.

MABEL. Lob's wood! I remember it all. We were here. We did go.

PURDIE. So we did. But how could . . . ? where was . . . ?

JOANNA. And who was . . . ?

MABEL. And what was . . . ?

PURDIE (*even in this supreme hour a man*). Don't let go. Hold on to what we were doing, or we shall lose grip of ourselves. Devotion. Something about devotion. Hold on to devotion. 'If the dog-like devotion of a lifetime . . .' Which of you was I saying that to?

MABEL. To me.

PURDIE. Are you sure?

MABEL (*shakily*). I am not quite sure.

PURDIE (*anxiously*). Joanna, what do you think? (*With a sudden increase of uneasiness.*) Which of you is my wife?

JOANNA (*without enthusiasm*). I am. No, I am not. It is Mabel who is your wife!

MABEL. Me?

PURDIE (*with a curious gulp*). Why, of course you are, Mabel!

MABEL. I believe I am!

PURDIE. And yet how can it be? I was running away with you.

JOANNA (*solving that problem*). You don't need to do it now.

PURDIE. The wood. Hold on to the wood.

The wood is what explains it. Yes, I see the whole thing. (*He gazes at* LOB.) You infernal old rascal! Let us try to think it out. Don't any one speak for a moment. Think first. Love . . . Hold on to love. (*He gets another tap*.) I say, I believe I am not a deeply passionate chap at all; I believe I am just . . . a philanderer!

MABEL. It is what you are,

JOANNA (*more magnanimous*). Mabel, what about ourselves?

PURDIE (*to whom it is truly a nauseous draught*). I didn't know. Just a philanderer! (*The soul of him would like at this instant to creep into another body*.) And if people don't change, I suppose we shall begin all over again now.

JOANNA (*the practical*). I daresay; but not with each other. I may philander again, but not with you.

(*They look on themselves without approval, always a sorry occupation. The man feels it most because he has admired himself most, or perhaps partly for some better reason*.)

PURDIE (*saying good-bye to an old friend*).

John Purdie, John Purdie, the fine fellow I used
to think you! (*When he is able to look them in
the face again.*) The wood has taught me one
thing, at any rate.

MABEL (*dismally*). What, Jack?

PURDIE. That it isn't accident that shapes
our lives.

JOANNA. No, it's Fate.

PURDIE (*the truth running through him, seeking
for a permanent home in him, willing to give him
still another chance, loth to desert him*). It's not
Fate, Joanna. Fate is something outside us.
What really plays the dickens with us is something in ourselves. Something that makes us
go on doing the same sort of fool things, however
many chances we get.

MABEL. Something in ourselves?

PURDIE (*shivering*). Something we are born
with.

JOANNA. Can't we cut out the beastly thing?

PURDIE. Depends, I expect, on how long we
have pampered him. We can at least control
him if we try hard enough. But I have for the
moment an abominably clear perception that the

likes of me never really tries. Forgive me, Joanna—no, Mabel—both of you. (*He is a shamed man.*) It isn't very pleasant to discover that one is a rotter. I suppose I shall get used to it.

JOANNA. I could forgive anybody anything to-night. (*Candidly.*) It is so lovely not to be married to you, Jack.

PURDIE (*spiritless*). I can understand that. I do feel small.

JOANNA (*the true friend*). You will soon swell up again.

PURDIE (*for whom, alas, we need not weep*). That is the appalling thing. But at present, at any rate, I am a rag at your feet, Joanna—no, at yours, Mabel. Are you going to pick me up? I don't advise it.

MABEL. I don't know whether I want to, Jack. To begin with, which of us is it your lonely soul is in search of?

JOANNA. Which of us is the fluid one, or the fluider one?

MABEL. Are you and I one? Or are you and Joanna one? Or are the three of us two?

JOANNA. He wants you to whisper in his ear, Mabel, the entrancing poem, 'Mabel Purdie.' Do it, Jack; there will be nothing wrong in it now.

PURDIE. Rub it in.

MABEL. When I meet Joanna's successor——

PURDIE (*quailing*). No, no, Mabel, none of that. At least credit me with having my eyes open at last. There will be no more of this. I swear it by all that is——

JOANNA (*in her excellent imitation of a sheep*). Baa-a, he is off again.

PURDIE. Oh Lord, so I am.

MABEL. Don't, Joanna.

PURDIE (*his mind still illumined*). She is quite right—I was. In my present state of depression —which won't last—I feel there is something in me that will make me go on being the same ass, however many chances I get. I haven't the stuff in me to take warning. My whole being is corroded. Shakespeare knew what he was talking about—

'The fault, dear Brutus, is not in our stars,
    But in ourselves, that we are underlings.'

JOANNA. For 'dear Brutus' we are to read 'dear audience' I suppose?

PURDIE. You have it.

JOANNA. Meaning that we have the power to shape ourselves?

PURDIE. We have the power right enough.

JOANNA. But isn't that rather splendid?

PURDIE. For those who have the grit in them, yes. (*Still seeing with a strange clearness through the chink the hammer has made.*) And they are not the dismal chappies; they are the ones with the thin bright faces. (*He sits lugubriously by his wife and is sorry for the first time that she has not married a better man.*) I am afraid there is not much fight in me, Mabel, but we shall see. If you catch me at it again, have the goodness to whisper to me in passing, 'Lob's Wood.' That may cure me for the time being.

MABEL (*still certain that she loved him once but not so sure why.*) Perhaps I will . . . as long as I care to bother, Jack. It depends on you how long that is to be.

JOANNA (*to break an awkward pause*). I feel that there is hope in that as well as a warning.

Perhaps the wood may prove to have been useful after all. (*This brighter view of the situation meets with no immediate response. With her next suggestion she reaches harbour.*) You know, we are not people worth being sorrowful about —so let us laugh.

> (*The ladies succeed in laughing though not prettily, but the man has been too much shaken.*)

JOANNA (*in the middle of her laugh*). We have forgotten the others! I wonder what is happening to them?

PURDIE (*reviving*). Yes, what about them? Have *they* changed!

MABEL. I didn't see any of them in the wood.

JOANNA. Perhaps we did see them without knowing them; we didn't know Lob.

PURDIE (*daunted*). That's true.

JOANNA. Won't it be delicious to be here to watch them when they come back, and see them waking up—or whatever it was we did.

PURDIE. What was it we did? I think something tapped me on the forehead.

MABEL (*blanching*). How do we know the others *will* come back?

JOANNA (*infected*). We don't know. How awful!

MABEL. Listen!

PURDIE. I distinctly hear some one on the stairs.

MABEL. It will be Matey.

PURDIE (*the chink beginning to close*). Be cautious both of you; don't tell him we have had any . . . odd experiences.

(*It is, however,* MRS. COADE *who comes down-stairs in a dressing-gown and carrying a candle and her husband's muffler.*)

MRS. COADE. So you are back at last. A nice house, I must say. Where is Coady?

PURDIE (*taken aback*). Coady! Did he go into the wood, too?

MRS. COADE (*placidly*). I suppose so. I have been down several times to look for him.

MABEL. Coady, too!

JOANNA (*seeing visions*). I wonder . . . Oh, how dreadful!

MRS. COADE. What is dreadful, Joanna?

JOANNA (*airily*). Nothing. I was just won-dering what he is doing.

MRS. COADE. Doing? What should he be doing? Did anything odd happen to you in the wood?

PURDIE (*taking command*). No, no, nothing.

JOANNA. We just strolled about, and came back. (*That subject being exhausted she points to* LOB.) Have you noticed him?

MRS. COADE. Oh, yes; he has been like that all the time. A sort of stupor, I think; and sometimes the strangest grin comes over his face.

PURDIE (*wincing*). Grin?

MRS. COADE. Just as if he were seeing amusing things in his sleep.

PURDIE (*guardedly*). I daresay he is. Oughtn't we to get Matey to him?

MRS. COADE. Matey has gone, too.

PURDIE. Wha-at!

MRS. COADE. At all events he is not in the house.

JOANNA (*unguardedly*). Matey! I wonder who is with him.

MRS. COADE. Must somebody be with him?

JOANNA. Oh, no, not at all.

(*They are simultaneously aware that some one outside has reached the window.*)

MRS. COADE. I hope it is Coady.

(*The other ladies are too fond of her to share this wish.*)

MABEL. Oh, I hope not.

MRS. COADE (*blissfully*). Why, Mrs. Purdie?

JOANNA (*coaxingly*). Dear Mrs. Coade, whoever he is, and whatever he does, I beg you not to be surprised. We feel that though we had no unusual experiences in the wood, others may not have been so fortunate.

MABEL. And be cautious, you dear, what you say to them before they come to.

MRS. COADE. 'Come to'? You puzzle me. And Coady didn't have his muffler.

(*Let it be recorded that in their distress for this old lady they forget their own misadventures.* PURDIE *takes a step toward the curtains in a vague desire to shield her;— and gets a rich reward; he has seen the coming addition to their circle.*)

PURDIE (*elated and pitiless*). It is Matey!

(*A butler intrudes who still thinks he is wrapped in fur.*)

JOANNA (*encouragingly*). Do come in.

MATEY. With apologies, ladies and gents. . . . May I ask who is host?

PURDIE (*splashing in the temperature that suits him best*). A very reasonable request. Third on the left.

MATEY (*advancing upon* LOB). Merely to ask, sir, if you can direct me to my hotel?

> (*The sleeper's only response is a slight quiver in one leg.*)

The gentleman seems to be reposing.

MRS. COADE. It is Lob.

MATEY. What is lob, ma'am?

MRS. COADE (*pleasantly curious*). Surely you haven't forgotten?

PURDIE (*over-riding her*). Anything we can do for you, sir? Just give it a name.

JOANNA (*in the same friendly spirit*). I hope you are not alone: do say you have some lady friends with you.

MATEY (*with an emphasis on his leading word*). My wife is with me.

JOANNA His wife! . . . (*With commendation.*) You *have* been quick!

MRS. COADE. I didn't know you were married.

MATEY. Why should you, madam? You talk as if you knew me.

MRS. COADE. Good gracious, do you really think I don't?

PURDIE (*indicating delicately that she is subject to a certain softening*). Sit down, won't you, my dear sir, and make yourself comfy.

MATEY (*accustomed of late to such deferential treatment*). Thank you. But my wife . . .

JOANNA (*hospitably*). Yes, bring her in; we are simply dying to make her acquaintance.

MATEY. You are very good; I am much obliged.

MABEL (*as he goes out*). Who can she be?

JOANNA (*leaping*). Who, who, who!

MRS. COADE. But what an extraordinary wood! He doesn't seem to know who he is at all.

MABEL (*soothingly*). Don't worry about that, Coady darling. He will know soon enough.

JOANNA (*again finding the bright side*). And so will the little wife! By the way, whoever she is, I hope she is fond of butlers.

MABEL (*who has peeped*). It is Lady Caroline!

JOANNA (*leaping again*). Oh, joy, joy! And she was so sure she couldn't take the wrong turning!

(*Lady Caroline is evidently still sure of it.*)

MATEY. May I present my wife—Lady Caroline Matey.

MABEL (*glowing*). How do you do!

PURDIE. Your servant, Lady Caroline.

MRS. COADE. Lady Caroline Matey! You?

LADY CAROLINE (*without an* r *in her*). Charmed, I 'm sure.

JOANNA (*neatly*). Very pleased to meet any wife of Mr. Matey.

PURDIE (*taking the floor*). Allow me. The Duchess of Candelabra. The Ladies Helena and Matilda M'Nab. I am the Lord Chancellor.

MABEL. I have wanted so long to make your acquaintance.

LADY CAROLINE. Charmed.

JOANNA (*gracefully*). These informal meetings are so delightful, don't you?

LADY CAROLINE. Yes, indeed.

MATEY (*the introductions being thus pleasantly concluded*). And your friend by the fire?

PURDIE. I will introduce you to him when you wake up—I mean when he wakes up.

MATEY. Perhaps I ought to have said that I am *James* Matey.

LADY CAROLINE (*the happy creature*). *The* James Matey.

MATEY. A name not, perhaps, unknown in the world of finance.

JOANNA. Finance? Oh, so you did take that clerkship in the City!

MATEY (*a little stiffly*). I began as a clerk in the City, certainly; and I am not ashamed to admit it.

MRS. COADE (*still groping*). Fancy that, now. And did it save you?

MATEY. Save me, madam?

JOANNA. Excuse us—we ask odd questions in this house; we only mean, did that keep you honest? Or are you still a pilferer?

LADY CAROLINE (*an outraged swan*). Husband mine, what does she mean?

JOANNA. No offence; I mean a pilferer on a large scale.

MATEY (*remembering certain newspaper jealousy*).

If you are referring to that Labrador business
—or the Working Women's Bank. . . .

PURDIE (*after the manner of one who has caught
a fly*). O-ho, got him!

JOANNA (*bowing*). Yes, those are what I
meant.

MATEY (*stoutly*). There was nothing proved.

JOANNA (*like one calling a meeting*). Mabel,
Jack, here is another of us! You have gone just
the same way again, my friend. (*Ecstatically.*)
There is more in it, you see, than taking the
wrong turning; you would always take the
wrong turning. (*The only fitting comment.*)
Tra-la-la!

LADY CAROLINE. If you are casting any
aspersions on my husband, allow me to say
that a prouder wife than I does not to-day
exist.

MRS. COADE (*who finds herself the only clear-
headed one*). My dear, do be careful.

MABEL. So long as you are satisfied, dear
Lady Caroline. But I thought you shrank from
all blood that was not blue.

LADY CAROLINE. You thought? Why should

you think about me? I beg to assure you
that I adore my Jim.

> (*She seeks his arm, but her* JIM *has encoun-
> tered the tray containing coffee cups and a
> cake, and his hands close on it with a cer-
> tain intimacy.*)

Whatever are you doing, Jim?

MATEY. I don't understand it, Caroliny;
but somehow I feel at home with this in my
hands.

MABEL. 'Caroliny!'

MRS. COADE. Look at me well; don't you
remember me?

MATEY (*musing*). I don't remember you;
but I seem to associate you with hard-boiled
eggs. (*With conviction.*) You like your eggs
hard-boiled.

PURDIE. Hold on to hard-boiled eggs! She
used to tip you especially to see to them.

> (MATEY'S *hand goes to his pocket.*)

Yes, that was the pocket.

LADY CAROLINE (*with distaste*). Tip!

MATEY (*without distaste*). Tip!

PURDIE. Jolly word, isn't it?

MATEY (*raising the tray*). It seems to set me thinking.

LADY CAROLINE (*feeling the tap of the hammer*). Why is my work-basket in this house?

MRS. COADE. You are living here, you know.

LADY CAROLINE. That is what a person feels. But when did I come? It is very odd, but one feels one ought to say when did one go.

PURDIE. She is coming to with a wush!

MATEY (*under the hammer*). Mr. . . . Purdie!

LADY CAROLINE. Mrs. Coade!

MATEY. The Guv'nor! My clothes!

LADY CAROLINE. One is in evening dress!

JOANNA (*charmed to explain*). You will understand clearly in a minute, Caroliny. You didn't really take that clerkship, Jim; you went into domestic service; but in the essentials you haven't altered.

PURDIE (*pleasantly*). I 'll have my shaving water at 7.30 sharp, Matey.

MATEY (*mechanically*). Very good, sir.

LADY CAROLINE. Sir? Midsummer Eve! The wood!

PURDIE. Yes, hold on to the wood.

MATEY. You are . . . you are . . . you are Lady Caroline Laney!

LADY CAROLINE. It is Matey, the butler!

MABEL. You seemed quite happy with him, you know, Lady Caroline.

JOANNA (*nicely*). We won't tell.

LADY CAROLINE (*subsiding*). Caroline Matey! And I seemed to like it! How horrible!

MRS. COADE (*expressing a general sentiment*). It is rather difficult to see what we should do next.

MATEY (*tentatively*). Perhaps if I were to go downstairs?

PURDIE. It would be conferring a personal favour on us all.

(*Thus encouraged* MATEY *and his tray resume friendly relations with the pantry.*)

LADY CAROLINE (*with itching fingers as she glares at* LOB). It is all that wretch's doing.

(*A quiver from* LOB'S *right leg acknowledges the compliment. The gay music of a pipe is heard from outside.*)

JOANNA (*peeping*). Coady!

MRS. COADE. Coady! Why is he so happy?

JOANNA (*troubled*). Dear, hold my hand.

MRS. COADE (*suddenly trembling*). Won't he know me?

PURDIE (*abashed by that soft face*). Mrs. Coade, I'm sorry. It didn't so much matter about the likes of us, but for your sake I wish Coady hadn't gone out.

MRS. COADE. We that have been happily married this thirty years.

COADE (*popping in buoyantly*). May I intrude? My name is Coade. The fact is I was playing about in the wood on a whistle, and I saw your light.

MRS. COADE (*the only one with the nerve to answer*). Playing about in the wood with a whistle!

COADE (*with mild dignity*). And why not, madam?

MRS. COADE. Madam! Don't you know me?

COADE. I don't know you. . . . (*Reflecting.*) But I wish I did.

MRS. COADE. Do you? Why?

COADE. If I may say so, you have a very soft, lovable face.

(*Several persons breathe again.*)

MRS. COADE (*inquisitorially*). Who was with you, playing whistles in the wood? (*The breathing ceases.*)

COADE. No one was with me.

(*And is resumed.*)

MRS. COADE. No . . . lady?

COADE. Certainly not. (*Then he spoils it.*) I am a bachelor.

MRS. COADE. A bachelor!

JOANNA. Don't give way, dear; it might be much worse.

MRS. COADE. A bachelor! And you are sure you never spoke to me before? Do think.

COADE. Not to my knowledge. Never . . . except in dreams.

MABEL (*taking a risk*). What did you say to her in dreams?

COADE. I said, 'My dear.' (*This when uttered surprises him.*) Odd!

JOANNA. The darling man!

MRS. COADE (*wavering*). How could you say such things to an old woman?

COADE (*thinking it out*). Old? I didn't think of you as old. No, no, young—with the morning dew on your face—coming across a lawn—in a black and green dress—and carrying such a pretty parasol.

MRS. COADE (*thrilling*). That was how he first met me! He used to love me in black and green; and it *was* a pretty parasol. Look, I am old. . . . So it can't be the same woman.

COADE (*blinking*). Old? Yes, I suppose so. But it is the same soft, lovable face, and the same kind, beaming smile that children could warm their hands at.

MRS. COADE. He always liked my smile.

PURDIE. So do we all.

COADE (*to himself*). Emma!

MRS. COADE. He hasn't forgotten my name!

COADE. It is sad that we didn't meet long ago. I think I have been waiting for you. I suppose we have met too late? You couldn't overlook my being an old fellow, could you, eh?

JOANNA. How lovely; he is going to propose to her again. Coady, you happy thing, he is wanting the same soft face after thirty years!

MRS. COADE (*undoubtedly hopeful*). We mustn't be too sure, but I think that is it.

(*Primly.*) What is it exactly that you want, Mr. Coade?

COADE (*under a lucky star*). I want to have the right to hold the parasol over you. Won't you be my wife, my dear, and so give my long dream of you a happy ending?

MRS. COADE (*preening*). Kisses are not called for at our age, Coady, but here is a muffler for your old neck.

COADE. My muffler; I have missed it. (*It is however to his forehead that his hand goes. Immediately thereafter he misses his sylvan attire.*) Why . . . why . . . what . . . who . . . how is this?

PURDIE (*nervously*). He is coming to.

COADE (*reeling and righting himself*). Lob!

(*The leg indicates that he has got it.*)

Bless me, Coady, I went into that wood!

MRS. COADE. And without your muffler, you that are so subject to chills. What are you feeling for in your pocket?

COADE. The whistle. It is a whistle I— Gone! of course it is. It's rather a pity. but . . . (*Anxious.*) Have I been saying awful things to you?

MABEL. You have been making her so proud. It is a compliment to our whole sex. You had a second chance, and it is her, again!

COADE. Of course it is. (*Crestfallen.*) But I see I was just the same nice old lazy Coady as before; and I had thought that if I had a second chance, I could do things. I have often said to you, Coady, that it was owing to my being cursed with a competency that I didn't write my great book. But I had no competency this time, and I haven't written a word.

PURDIE (*bitterly enough*). That needn't make you feel lonely in this house.

MRS. COADE (*in a small voice*). You seem to have been quite happy as an old bachelor, dear.

COADE. I am surprised at myself, Emma, but I fear I was.

MRS. COADE (*with melancholy perspicacity*). I wonder if what it means is that you don't especially need even me. I wonder if it means that you are just the sort of amiable creature that would be happy anywhere, and anyhow?

COADE. Oh dear, can it be as bad as that!

JOANNA (*a ministering angel she*). Certainly

not. It is a romance, and I won't have it looked upon as anything else.

MRS. COADE. Thank you, Joanna. You will try not to miss that whistle, Coady?

COADE (*getting the footstool for her*). You are all I need.

MRS. COADE. Yes; but I am not so sure as I used to be that it is a great compliment.

JOANNA. Coady, behave.

(*There is a knock on the window.*)

PURDIE (*peeping*). Mrs. Dearth! (*His spirits revive.*) She is alone. Who would have expected that of *her!*

MABEL. She is a wild one, Jack, but I sometimes thought rather a dear; I do hope she has got off cheaply.

(ALICE *comes to them in her dinner gown.*)

PURDIE (*the irrepressible*). Pleased to see you, stranger.

ALICE (*prepared for ejection.*) I was afraid such an unceremonious entry might startle you.

PURDIE. Not a bit.

ALICE (*defiant*). I usually enter a house by the front door.

PURDIE. I have heard that such is the swagger way.

ALICE (*simpering*). So stupid of me. I lost myself in the wood . . . and . . .

JOANNA (*genially*). Of course you did. But never mind that; do tell us your name.

LADY CAROLINE (*emerging again*). Yes, yes, your name.

ALICE. Of course, I am the Honourable Mrs. Finch-Fallowe.

LADY CAROLINE. Of course, of course!

PURDIE. I hope Mr. Finch-Fallowe is very well? We don't know him personally, but may we have the pleasure of seeing him bob up presently?

ALICE. No, I am not sure where he is.

LADY CAROLINE (*with point*). I wonder if the dear clever police know?

ALICE (*imprudently*). No, they don't.

(*It is a very secondary matter to her. This woman of calamitous fires hears and sees her tormentors chiefly as the probable owners of the cake which is standing on that tray.*)

So awkward, I gave my sandwiches to a poor

girl and her father whom I met in the wood, and
now . . . isn't it a nuisance—I am quite
hungry. (*So far with a mincing bravado.*)
May I?

> (*Without waiting for consent she falls to upon
> the cake, looking over it like one ready to
> fight them for it.*)

PURDIE (*sobered again*). Poor soul.

LADY CAROLINE. We are so anxious to know
whether you met a friend of ours in the
wood—a Mr. Dearth.   Perhaps you know him,
too?

ALICE. Dearth?   I don't know any Dearth.

MRS. COADE. Oh dear, what a wood!

LADY CAROLINE. He is quite a front door sort
of man; knocks and rings, you know.

PURDIE. Don't worry her.

ALICE (*gnawing*). I meet so many; you see
I go out a great deal.   I have visiting-cards—
printed ones.

LADY CAROLINE. How very distingué. Perhaps Mr. Dearth has painted your portrait; he
is an artist.

ALICE. Very likely; they all want to paint

me. I daresay that is the man to whom I gave
my sandwiches.

MRS. COADE. But I thought you said he had
a daughter?

ALICE. Such a pretty girl; I gave her half a
crown.

COADE. A daughter? That can't be Dearth.

PURDIE (*darkly*). Don't be too sure. Was the
man you speak of a rather chop-fallen, gone-to-
seed sort of person.

ALICE. No, I thought him such a jolly,
attractive man.

COADE. Dearth jolly, attractive! oh no.
Did he say anything about his wife?

LADY CAROLINE. Yes, do try to remember if he
mentioned her.

ALICE (*snapping*). No, he didn't.

PURDIE. He was far from jolly in her time.

ALICE (*with an archness for which the cake is
responsible*). Perhaps that was the lady's fault.

(*The last of the adventurers draws nigh,
carolling a French song as he comes.*)

COADE. Dearth's voice. He sounds quite
merry!

JOANNA (*protecting*). Alice, you poor thing.

PURDIE. This is going to be horrible.

(*A clear-eyed man of lusty gait comes in.*)

DEARTH. I am sorry to bounce in on you in this way, but really I have an excuse. I am a painter of sorts, and . . .

> (*He sees he has brought some strange discomfort here.*)

MRS. COADE. I must say, Mr. Dearth, I am delighted to see you looking so well. Like a new man, isn't he?

(*No one dares to answer.*)

DEARTH. I am certainly very well, if you care to know. But did I tell you my name?

JOANNA (*for some one has to speak*). No, but—but we have an instinct in this house.

DEARTH. Well, it doesn't matter. Here is the situation; my daughter and I have just met in the wood a poor woman famishing for want of food. We were as happy as grigs ourselves, and the sight of her distress rather cut us up. Can you give me something for her? Why are you looking so startled? (*Seeing the remains of the cake.*) May I have this?

(*A shrinking movement from one of them
draws his attention, and he recognises in
her the woman of whom he has been speaking. He sees her in fine clothing and he
grows stern.*)

I feel I can't be mistaken; it was you I met
in the wood? Have you been playing some
trick on me? (*To the others.*) It was for her I
wanted the food.

ALICE (*her hand guarding the place where his
gift lies*). Have you come to take back the
money you gave me?

DEARTH. Your dress! You were almost in
rags when I saw you outside.

ALICE (*frightened as she discovers how she is
now attired*). I don't . . . understand . . .

COADE (*gravely enough*). For that matter,
Dearth, I daresay you were different in the wood,
too.

(DEARTH *sees his own clothing.*)

DEARTH. What . . . !

ALICE (*frightened*). Where am I? (*To* MRS.
COADE.) I seem to know you . . . do I?

MRS. COADE (*motherly*). Yes, you do; hold

my hand, and you will soon remember all about it.

JOANNA. I am afraid, Mr. Dearth, it is harder for you than for the rest of us.

PURDIE (*looking away*). I wish I could help you, but I can't; I am a rotter.

MABEL. We are awfully sorry. Don't you remember . . . Midsummer Eve?

DEARTH (*controlling himself*). Midsummer Eve? This room. Yes, this room. . . . You . . . was it you? . . . were going out to look for something. . . . The tree of knowledge, wasn't it? Somebody wanted me to go, too. . . . Who was that? A lady, I think. . . . Why did she ask me to go? What was I doing here? I was smoking a cigar. . . . I laid it down, there. . . . (*He finds the cigar.*) Who was the lady?

ALICE (*feebly*). Something about a second chance.

MRS. COADE. Yes, you poor dear, you thought you could make so much of it.

DEARTH. A lady who didn't like me—(*With conviction.*) She had good reasons, too—but what were they . . . ?

ALICE. A little old man! He did it. What did he do?

(*The hammer is raised.*)

DEARTH. I am . . . it is coming back—I am not the man I thought myself.

ALICE. I am not Mrs. Finch-Fallowe. Who am I?

DEARTH (*staring at her*). You were that lady.

ALICE. It is you—my husband!

(*She is overcome.*)

MRS. COADE. My dear, you are much better off, so far as I can see, than if you were Mrs. Finch-Fallowe.

ALICE (*with passionate knowledge*). Yes, yes indeed! (*Generously.*) But he isn't.

DEARTH. Alice! . . . I—(*He tries to smile.*) I didn't know you when I was in the wood with Margaret. She . . . she . . . Margaret . . .

(*The hammer falls.*)

O my God!

(*He buries his face in his hands.*)

ALICE. I wish—I wish——

(*She presses his shoulder fiercely and then stalks out by the door.*)

PURDIE (*to* LOB, *after a time*). You old ruffian.

DEARTH. No, I am rather fond of him, our lonely, friendly little host. Lob, I thank thee for that hour.

(*The seedy-looking fellow passes from the scene.*)

COADE. Did you see that his hand is shaking again?

PURDIE. The watery eye has come back.

JOANNA. And yet they are both quite nice people.

PURDIE (*finding the tragedy of it*). We are all quite nice people.

MABEL. If she were not such a savage!

PURDIE. I daresay there is nothing the matter with her except that she would always choose the wrong man, good man or bad man, but the wrong man for her.

COADE. We can't change.

MABEL. Jack says the brave ones can.

JOANNA. 'The ones with the thin bright faces.'

MABEL. Then there is hope for you and me, Jack.

PURDIE (*ignobly*). I don't expect so.

JOANNA (*wandering about the room, like one renewing acquaintance with it after returning from a journey*). Hadn't we better go to bed? it must be getting late.

PURDIE. Hold on to bed! (*They all brighten.*)

MATEY (*entering*). Breakfast is quite ready.

(*They exclaim.*)

LADY CAROLINE. My watch has stopped.

JOANNA. And mine. Just as well perhaps!

MABEL. There is a smell of coffee.

(*The gloom continues to lift.*)

COADE. Come along, Coady; I do hope you have not been tiring your foot.

MRS. COADE. I shall give it a good rest to-morrow, dear.

MATEY. I have given your egg six minutes, ma'am.

> (*They set forth once more upon the eternal round. The curious* JOANNA *remains behind.*)

JOANNA. A strange experiment, Matey; does it ever have any permanent effect?

MATEY (*on whom it has had none*). So far as I

know, not often, miss; but, I believe, once in a while.

> (*There is hope in this for the brave ones. If we could wait long enough we might see the* DEARTHS *breasting their way into the light.*)

He could tell you.

> (*The elusive person thus referred to kicks responsively, meaning perhaps that none of the others will change till there is a tap from another hammer. But when* MATEY *goes to rout him from his chair he is no longer there. His disappearance is no shock to* MATEY, *who shrugs his shoulders and opens the windows to let in the glory of a summer morning. The garden has returned, and our queer little hero is busy at work among his flowers. A lark is rising.*)

The End